The Female Fan
GUIDE TO MOTORSPORTS
by Betsy Berns

For Drew

The Female Fan Guide to Motorsports

By Betsy Berns

Published by: **BVision Sportsmedia, L.P.**
303 E. 57th St.
New York, NY 10022

ISBN 0-9653882-4-7

Disclaimer:
The author and publisher have made every effort to ensure accuracy of data, however, there may be typographical or content related errors. This text is intended as a general guide and not as the ultimate motorsports authority.

The Female Fan Guide to Sports series
Quick, easy, educational, and fun guides to your favorite sports.

CONTENTS

Acknowledgments

I'd like to thank the following people for helping me piece together the information necessary for writing this book.

Many thanks goes to Kathi Lauterbach of Newman Haas Racing, Tara Martorana of CART, Andy Papathanassiou, Shaun Assael, Christian Fittipaldi, Lyn St. James, Lesley Visser, Chris Visser, Sam Wyche, Joe Gibbs Racing and Cindi Magnum, Jennifer Tumminelli, Jennifer Karpf of the National Sports Marketing Network, Peter Baron, Elizabeth Daliere, Ted Peters, Lynne Tapper, David Suber, Guy Courtney, Rob Tuckman, Bill Scovin, Lenny Passarelli at Bobby Van's, Lisa McCaffrey and Julie Romanowski.

Editors: Ward Woodbury, D. Robert Korn

Cover Design: Kurt Metzler, Metzler Design and Christi Finger, GMR Marketing

Book Design and Layout: Kurt Metzler, Metzler Design

Author Photos: Jonathan Ressler

Photos courtesy of Newman Haas Racing, Dan R Incorporated Photography, Motor Sport Images, Joe Gibbs Racing, Chobat Racing Images, Lyn St. James Racing, International Speedway Corporation/NASCAR, Daytona Racing Archives, Championship Auto Racing Teams, Inc. and Allsport USA.

Foreword

BY LYN ST. JAMES
1992 INDY 500
ROOKIE OF THE YEAR

Motorsports seems to be perceived by so many as a "man's" sport, which I do not agree with. It's just that more men than women over the years have been attracted to the sport. I've been actively involved in the sport for over 25 years and have rarely felt unwelcome. There certainly have been times when I've wanted to respond to actions or comments that bothered me, but when I gave it a rational thought I always end up with the same decision; it's not worth it. It's so much fun, so challenging, so full of interesting people who are unique individuals that have a common love: racing. Just because men have dominated the sport for so long doesn't mean that women are not wanted. In fact, I believe it's one of the few sports

Lyn St. James

where women can contribute and compete on equal ground. But as in all endeavors, knowledge is power. So all you have to do is learn the lingo, learn the principles, and understand that everyone in this sport is passionate about it. It's difficult to be a casual fan or participant. Racing just brings out the intensity in everything and everyone. It demands 100% of the horsepower possible, whether it's human or mechanical. So read it, learn about it, and come on in because it's a great ride.

Lyn St. James

Preface

WELCOME TO MOTORSPORTS

The book is divided into laps, just like a race. Like my other Female Fan Guides, the book includes fun facts, helpful hints, interviews and graphics for an easy and entertaining read.

During the first few laps you get up to speed by learning the difference between CART, NASCAR, IRL and Formula One racing. You then speed up and learn the history of NASCAR and the divisions that comprise the NASCAR circuit.

Now you are cruising as you learn about the anatomy of a stock car, the importance of the pit crew, the flags and the rules.

During pit stops, you will read about the training requirements, preparation and stress levels of the pit crew from a crew chief, pit crew trainer and pit crew member.

The race is really heating up now, and you need to know about the most famous races in NASCAR history, the road to the Winston Cup Championships, and the excitement of Race Day.

Just a few laps from the finish line, you learn a little about the open wheel series CART, including history, interview with a driver, road to the FedEx championship and the differences between CART and IRL.

You have now captured the checkered flag and will be ready to head to the tracks and enjoy your experience.

LAP ONE
THE GREEN FLAG

AN INTRODUCTION TO
MOTORSPORTS

Professional Auto Racing hasn't been around as long as other "stick and ball" sports such as football, baseball, soccer, etc. However, car racing does have a rich and interesting history.

Auto racing takes many forms, based on the size, shape and type of vehicle as well as distance and racing surface. All share certain things in common, the roar of the engine, the smell of burning rubber and exhaust fumes, the heart-pounding excitement, the blazing speeds, and the thrill of watching the checkered flag come down.

Whether or not you're a motorsports fan, you may be confused by all of the different types of races and race cars. Don't worry about remembering every truck, go-kart, drag and midget car series. You'll drive yourself crazy. The most important thing to keep straight in the professional ranks is the difference between open-wheel racing and stock car racing. While you'll find many race fans that love both stock car and open-wheel, you'll also hear fans who adamantly and vocally support one type of series over the other.

Following this introduction, The Female Fan Guide to Motorsports will focus on the two most popular forms of racing in the U.S., stock car racing (NASCAR) and the open-wheel circuits (CART and IRL). Every series has its own special qualities, however, so explore the similarities and differences and have fun whether you're a newly converted fan or a seasoned veteran of the NASCAR infield.

Here's a quick guide to the differences between the major racing series.

In General...

Open-wheel racing is what it sounds like - the wheels are exposed. The cars have big, oversized tires that stick out of the fuselage. The cars are long and cigar shaped, and ride very close to the ground. These cars are built for speed, and there's no risk of confusing them with your father's Oldsmobile. Open wheel racing includes Indy Racing League (IRL), Formula One and Championship Auto Racing Teams (CART).

> **FUN FACT**
>
> As of the 1999 season, Michael Schumacher of Formula One racing was one of the highest paid, if not the highest paid, athletes in the world.

Stock cars, on the other hand, look similar to everyday street cars. In fact, these cars captured America's attention in part because they appear similar to the cars many Americans drive on a daily basis. Under the hood, of course, a NASCAR racer has as much in common with your three-year-old Ford Taurus as an F-16 fighter plane has with a commuter jet. Stock car racing in the U.S. is dominated by the National Association for Stock Car Auto Racing (NASCAR).

Motorsports Overview...

Formula One (international open wheel racing)

Formula One (F1) is also known as Grand Prix racing and is considered second to soccer as the most popular sport in the world. Founded in 1950, The Federation Internationale de l'Automobile (FIA) currently sanctions the Formula One Championship Series. The races, all of which are held on irregularly-shaped road courses, take place in venues all over Europe, Latin America and Southeast Asia. The United States used to host Formula One racing, but hasn't held a race since 1991.

Formula One cars are considered the fastest racing cars in the world, with the most sophisticated technology. Formula One racing requires massive sums of money to support the cars, of which you'll see, among other top brands, Ferraris and Mercedes Benz. The cost of operating a top Formula One team for a year has escalated dramatically to over 50 million dollars.

HELPFUL HINT

If you're an American with an interest in Formula One, stay tuned. Formula One racing is due back in the United States in 2000 at the Indianapolis Motor Speedway.

CART and the IRL (U.S. open-wheel racing)

Championship Auto Racing Teams (CART) and the Indy Racing League (IRL) used to be one series called IndyCar racing. But in 1995, due to a series of disagreements, the league split and became two separate entities. (For more information on the split and the differences between the two series, see "History of CART" chapter and "Pit Stop, CART vs. IRL.")

FUN FACT

According to CART, more than 60 million people in 188 countries watch each race.

The cars used in both series look very similar to Formula One cars. But don't confuse F1 with any form of Indy Car racing or you're bound to offend the hard-

CART open-wheel racing

core Formula One fan. Formula One cars have more sophisticated technology (and cost significantly more money).

HELPFUL HINT

The cars that race in CART are called Champ Cars, and the cars that race in the IRL are called Indy Cars.

If you're still confused about Indy Cars (IRL) and Champ cars (CART), the simplest way to remember the difference is this: CART inherited the most well known drivers, while the IRL inherited the most famous race, the Indianapolis 500. The other major difference is that CART can run races on oval tracks and road courses, while the IRL runs strictly on ovals.

There is a possibility that the two leagues will merge again to become one open-wheel racing league in the U.S. That would certainly make things less complicated for American racing fans.

NASCAR (stock car racing)

In recent years, NASCAR (National Association for Stock Car Auto Racing) surged in popularity to become one of the fastest growing and most popular sports in America. NASCAR had its origins in early stock car racing in the south during the 1920's. (For more information on NASCAR, see the chapter "History of NASCAR.")

NASCAR racing

Stock cars look similar to, and are based on, American made cars. The NASCAR Winston Cup Series is the most competitive and prestigious series within NASCAR, and its headline event, the Daytona 500, is considered the Super Bowl of stock car racing, becoming one of the most watched sporting events in the world.

There is a "down side" to higher speeds...

LAP 2
Moonshine to Millionaires
THE HISTORY OF NASCAR

Auto racing has experienced a huge surge in popularity in recent years, despite some fundamental disadvantages versus other stick and ball sports. Stock car racing hasn't been around as long, children don't grow up playing it in their backyards, it's not a playground sport and there are no college scholarships.

Stock car racing has a rich an intriguing history dating back to prohibition. During America's roaring twenties, alcohol, which was (seemingly) scarce, commanded a high premium if it was delivered promptly and secretly. A fast, renegade driver could become famous for running moonshine (so called because the alcohol was often delivered late at night, by the light of the moon, so the drivers would have less chance of getting caught) from the "stills" to various points of distribution. During, and even after prohibition, these drivers boasted of their driving prowess and became local celebrities. With bragging rights on the line and testosterone flowing, drivers continually challenged each other to determine the best drivers in the region. These challenges led to informal races, which, more often than not, were disorganized and fraudulent. Back then, if you had suggested that such races would lead to an organized sport, you would have been laughed out of town.

Then, along came a gentleman named William Henry Getty France (known later as "Big Bill"). In 1934, Big Bill and his wife, Anne, wanted to seek out a better style of living, so they took a chance, left their home in Washington, D.C., and headed south. Bill's goal was to get a job as an auto mechanic in the warm confines of Miami, Florida. Big Bill figured that in Florida, he could work on cars (which he loved to do) in a pleasant tropical setting. On the way to Miami, Bill's car broke down in Daytona Beach. Bill apparently liked what he saw of Daytona and decided to take a job in the garage of a Pontiac-Cadillac dealership. He set up shop and, in his spare time, did a little racing on one of the local circuits. Unfortunately, the operators of these races shared little of the fledgling sport's revenues with the drivers.

FUN FACT

In 1940, Big Bill France held the National Stock Car Champion title.

Unhappy with the way things were run, Bill joined forces with his friend, Charlie Reese (a restaurant owner), to promote and operate races. After marginal success in their early efforts, they found a formula that could attract enough quality drivers and enough fans to turn a profit.

Among their greatest challenges was how to annoint a champion. Like boxing today or college football before the recent adoption of the Bowl Championship Series (See The Female Fan Guide to Pro Football), the process for determining a stock car champion had become confusing and contentious. At the time, any race car driver who won a race would claim to be a champion. In order to make the title meaningful and therefore valuable, the sport had to establish an agreed-upon set of rules and regulations. France believed that if he standardized the sport, added rules, a set schedule of events and a point system to award a winner for the series, he could make car racing more of a national phenomenon.

FUN FACT

Red Byron won the first NASCAR season title in 1949. As a former war hero, whose shoe had to be bolted to the clutch, he was an immediate fan favorite.

On December 14, 1947, Bill France assembled a group of 35 men in the Ebony Bar at Daytona Beach's Streamline Hotel. While puffing away on cigars, they began to discuss the future of stock car racing. Out of a series of discussions that began that day, the National Association for Stock Car Auto Racing (NASCAR) was born on February 21, 1948. Big Bill was, naturally, elected president of the association and given the authority to determine the type of races to be run. Big Bill had the foresight to predict that the average driver and fan would be more interested in racing if he could identify with the cars. He felt that the cars should look like, and be modeled after, standard passenger cars from the factories. This way, fans could identify with the cars, and the races would profile and emphasize the skills of the drivers rather than the mechanical superiority of the machines.

Of course, the best laid plans often go awry. The first race under the new rules was to have required that all drivers race full-size American cars ("strictly stock") for the championship title. Unfortunately, World War II prevented production of new car models, so the first race in 1948 ran with "modified" prewar automobiles.

By the 1949 season, the war had ended, automobile production rebounded and full-size "strictly stock" cars became readily available. Charlotte Motor Speedway (recently renamed Lowe's Motor Speedway) hosted the first Strictly Stock race, later known as the Grand National Division. The first race was controversial. Initially, an unknown driver named Glenn Dunnaway was crowned the winner, but Dunnaway was later disqualified for having illegal modifications to his car, and the runner-up, Jim Roper, is listed as the official winner of the event.

As with other major sports, winnings have changed dramatically over the years. The winner of the first NASCAR Strictly Stock race received just $2,000 and all of the other drivers split a whopping $1,000.

By 1950, races were springing up all around the southern part of the U.S. That year, the first 500-mile race for stock cars took place at Darlington (S.C.) Raceway, the first superspeedway built for stock cars. Darlington's Southern 500 celebrated its 50th anniversary in 1999, which makes it one of the oldest tracks on the NASCAR tour. To this day, it's still one of the toughest. The track is egg-shaped rather than a true oval, and is considered one of the most difficult tracks to maneuver. As more and more track owners saw the benefits of holding races, the schedule expanded from eight races in 1949 to 45 races in 1955.

Even though the number of races multiplied and the events started to draw more fans and plenty of drivers, in its early years NASCAR was still not a cohesive organization. There were no formal marketing and public relations efforts at that time. Many of the drivers, however, tried to bring their own form of marketing and public relations to the sport through colorful behavior (See Fun Fact on the next page). The Flock brothers (Tim, Bob and Fonty), Curtis Turner, Lee Petty, Ned Jarrett and Junior Johnson were making names for themselves both as drivers and as entertaining personalities.

FUN FACT

You can't blame Glenn Dunnaway for being disqualified. When he showed up at the track the day of the race, he was hoping to find a car to race. Car owner Hubert Westmoreland was looking for a driver, and the two agreed on the spot to team up.

FUN FACT

Sara Christian was the first female driver to race in a NASCAR race. She raced on June 19, 1949, at Charlotte Motor Speedway

HELPFUL HINT

Darlington's Southern 500 takes place every year on Labor Day Weekend.

Big Bill never strayed from his mission of bringing stock car racing to the forefront of the American sports scene. He knew that to achieve maximum success, the sport needed to present a reputable image to the public, and he took steps to preserve that image. For example, when his good friend and fellow racer, Curtis Turner took out a loan from the (less than "squeaky clean") Teamsters Union to finance construction of Charlotte Motor Speedway, he suspended Turner from racing and any involvement with NASCAR for four years. This tough stance sent a message to other owners, drivers and potential participants: Don't mess with NASCAR.

FUN FACT

Tim Flock saw the need to add more "jazz" to racing. So, in 1952, he raced with a monkey named Jocko Flocko by his side. Jocko didn't understand the responsibilities of riding shotgun, however, and during one race, he decided it would be fun to climb on Tim's shoulders. Needless to say, that was Jocko's last race.

HELPFUL HINT

Even though Curtis Turner was in Big Bill's penalty box for four years, he is still considered one of the greatest drivers in the history of the sport.

American-made cars were the norm in NASCAR, with Ford and Chrysler representing most of the field. These manufacturers worked at making the cars faster and faster, and saw significant increases in sales due to the cars' performances.

With racing speeds accelerating, some drivers started to worry about their safety. Richard Petty, one of the greatest drivers of all time, took it upon himself to organize the Professional Drivers Association (PDA). When members of the PDA refused to show up for a race at Talladega, NASCAR got nervous. Big Bill was completely undaunted, however, and at 59 years of age, jumped into a car and drove 176 mph for a few laps around the track to demonstrate the safety of the track at the aggressive speeds. The PDA went out of business shortly after Big Bill's gutsy move.

From Strictly Stock to Winston Cup...

Despite the safety measures required by NASCAR, such as drivers wearing helmets and being strapped into their cars, NASCAR still suffered some negative publicity. In fact, the 1960s proved to be a decade of controversy and challenges for NASCAR. Three major celebrities of the decade - Fireball Roberts, Jimmy Pardue and Joe Weatherly - died in racing accidents. Then the unthinkable happened. Ford and Chrysler decided to discontinue contributing the significant amounts of money they had been providing to competitors, ending a much-needed financial relationship. Who knew at the time that this disappointment would bring on a whole new era of corporate sponsorship?

HELPFUL HINT

Among the American-made brands of cars allowed on the NASCAR circuit were not only Ford and Chrysler, but also Cadillac, Buick, Chevrolet, Lincoln, Kaiser, Mercury and Oldsmobile.

Desperately needing sponsorship money, Junior Johnson journeyed to Winston-Salem, N.C., to convince executives at R.J. Reynolds to invest $700,000-800,000 dollars in his race team. Ralph Seagraves, the special event director at R.J. Reynolds, immediately saw the potential of an RJR-NASCAR association and pushed to extend the relationship beyond just investing in a particular team. RJR needed to find alternative ways to promote its Winston brand of cigarettes, since tobacco had been forbidden from commercial advertising on television.

RJR jumped into this now long-standing relationship by title sponsoring the Grand National Series, which included distributing money into a special points fund for the teams and drivers, as well as investing in various promotional activities. In 1972, the previously named NASCAR Grand National Series officially became what we all know today as the NASCAR Winston Cup Series. Sponsoring NASCAR allowed RJR to get its major brand name, Winston, in front of millions of TV viewers and race attendees.

By the mid-1970s, the reigns of NASCAR shifted from Bill France Sr., to his son, Bill Jr. There is no question that Big Bill was a dominant and important figure in the emergence of NASCAR as a sport, but his son, William Clifton France (Bill Jr.), transformed NASCAR from a regional sport to a national pastime. Bill Jr. applied sophisticated marketing techniques to entice corporate sponsors to pour millions of dollars into the sport. Bill Jr. was certainly one of the reasons for the immense growth and popularity of NASCAR.

Many sports have one moment in their history that fans can point to as the pivotal event that changed the nature of the sport. In NASCAR history, it would have to be the 1979 Daytona 500. This was the first 500-mile race to be televised live. And, as fate would have it, a huge snowstorm enveloped much of the country the day of the race. This "act of God" left thousands of people at home with nothing to do but watch TV ... and lo and behold, what did they turn on? Five hundred miles of live NASCAR racing.

This was no boring 500-miles, either, particularly the last lap. Donnie Allison and Cale Yarborough were racing head to head on the last lap when their cars crashed, spinning them out of control. Richard Petty ended up winning the race, but the real drama came when Donnie Allison's brother (Bobby) came over to Donnie to see if he was okay. Tensions flared and Donnie and Bobby got into a fistfight with Cale Yarborough. As we all know, the American public loves drama and excitement, and this was just what the sport needed to convince viewers that racing incited passion and intensity among its drivers. These guys weren't just boring drivers, they were passionate teammates, brothers and sports figures. (For more on this race, see the Chapter on Memorable Moments.)

Richard Petty, winner of the famous 1979 Daytona 500 and 199 other Winston Cup races.

There were many significant events during the early years of racing. For one, a car drove over 200 mph - faster than fans once suspected possible. The major draws during this era, however, were the drivers themselves. Among the NASCAR legends racing the circuits every week were Richard Petty, Cale Yarborough, Darrell Waltrip, David Pearson, Dale Earnhardt and Bobby Allison.

HELPFUL HINT

Refer to Richard Petty as "The King" and refer to David Pearson as "The Silver Fox". Both retired, these two drivers hold the record for Winston Cup wins, Petty won an amazing 200 races, while Pearson won 105.

Unlike most other sports with multiple team owners sharing in cooperative leagues, NASCAR is still 100% owned by the France family. Numerous members of the France family have made major contributions to the sport and have been responsible for its rising success. The late Bill France Sr. still deserves recognition for his innovation, creativity and guts. He took the concept of a dirt race with former moonshiners and made it one of the most popular and fastest-growing sports of this century. What a legacy!

FUN FACT

Richard Petty holds many of stock car racing's most important records. These include:

Races started: 1,184

Races won: 200

Top 5 Finishes: 555

Poles: 126

Laps completed: 307,836

Laps led: 52, 194

Consecutive races won: 10 (1967)

Consecutive years racing 35 (1958-1992)

Petty won seven Winston Cups, in 1964, 1967, 1971, 1972, 1974, 1975 and 1979. It is unlikely that any racer will ever rival Richard Petty's dominance of this sport during his years at the top.

Bobby Allison

LAP 3
NASCAR
IT'S MORE
THAN JUST THE CUP

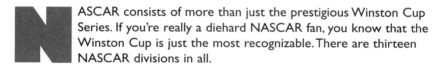

ASCAR consists of more than just the prestigious Winston Cup Series. If you're really a diehard NASCAR fan, you know that the Winston Cup is just the most recognizable. There are thirteen NASCAR divisions in all.

Here's an easy guideline to follow all NASCAR sanctioned events to avoid confusion as to which race you've just turned on.

The Premier Division - NASCAR Winston Cup Series

This series is considered the major league of stock car racing. It is the most recognized and most prestigious of all the divisions. The season includes 34 points races. This means that of the 36 events run per year, only 34 of those count toward points in the Winston Cup Series championship. Currently, twenty-one tracks hold Winston Cup events. If you're a track owner, it's considered very prestigious and profitable to have a Winston Cup race.

NASCAR Busch Series, Grand National Division

Think of Triple-A in baseball. Most drivers with Winston Cup aspirations will compete in the Busch Series to test and develop their abilities. These are top flight professional drivers who have risen almost to the peak of their profession but who lack experience, track record, or financial backing to compete at the Winston Cup level. Since the cars in the Busch Series are very similar to Winston Cup cars, drivers can get a good gauge as to how they would fare in the "big leagues." The Grand National division has been sponsored by the venerable brewing company Anheuser-Busch since 1982.

HELPFUL HINT

While the cars in the Busch Series and the Winston Cup Series look similar, there's actually a difference. Busch cars weigh 100 pounds less, measure five inches shorter and have slightly less horsepower than Winston Cup cars do.

FUN FACT

Homerun King Mark McGwire invested in the Hillin Racing team, where driver Bobby Hillin Jr. competed in the 1998 Busch Series.

NASCAR Craftsman Truck Series

Unlike Busch, there's little risk of confusing the Craftsman Truck Series with Winston Cup. Yes, you guessed it, this Series is made up of Trucks. And, not just any trucks. These trucks are full-sized pickup trucks modified for racing.

THE REGIONAL TOURING DIVISIONS

Regional Touring Divisions, ten in all, are distinguished based on type of vehicle, level of driver skill, and in some cases, geography. These are the equivalent of AA and A minor leagues in baseball — professional and exciting, but a few notches below the majors. Each has its own sponsor and its own, often regional, but very loyal base of fans.

Winston West Series

Think old and west. This series has been around since 1954 and has tracks located predominately on the West Coast. You'll see tracks in California, Arizona, Colorado, Nevada, Washington, Oregon and Arizona.

Busch North Series

This series features cars that are similar to the Busch Series. In fact, many drivers graduate from here to compete in the Busch Series, Grand National Division (and then, of course, on to Winston Cup).

Busch All-Star Series

Dirt tracks are the norm in the Midwest, so all of these races are on dirt.

Featherlite Modified Series

This is racing's oldest series. It's run mostly in the Northeast and features open-wheel (or fender-free, if you want to be precise) cars.

Featherlite Southwest Series

You'll find these races in the Southwest. These cars have sedan-style bodies.

Slim Jim All-Pro Series

This series takes place primarily in the Southeast and is very similar to the Featherlite Modified Series.

Goody's Dash Series

The Goody's Dash Series serves as a good starting place for drivers. The cars race on four-cylinder engines on both short tracks and superspeedways.

> **FUN FACT**
>
> If you're having dreams of driving at Daytona, but don't want to work your way through the system, check out a race car simulator. You'll feel as though you're right there on the track, but thankfully, you won't hurt anyone. You can find one of these cool attractions at the Mall of the Americas in Minneapolis, as well as in Chicago, Dallas and Irvine, Calif.

Raybestos Brakes Northwest Series

Just think Slim Jim All-Pro Series, but in the Northwest.

RE/MAX Challenge Series

This new NASCAR series is for race fans who live in the upper Midwest.

NASCAR Weekly Racing Series

This is the grassroots backbone of racing for fans across the country. With approximately 100 short tracks around the nation, drivers compete regionally with the opportunity for national recognition as well.

The Winston Cup is the premiere NASCAR series

LAP 4

The Anatomy of a Stock Car & the Tracks

The lure and popularity of NASCAR can be traced largely to the car. When Big Bill France decided to introduce racing to the masses, he specifically wanted the cars to look like the type of American-made cars driven by everyday folks. He correctly assumed that if people could identify with the cars, they would, in some way, identify more with the races. He also wanted the focus to be on the drivers and their abilities. He may or may not have realized the other added benefit of this strategy: the car manufacturers falling over themselves to produce quality racing machines that did well enough on the tracks to induce purchases in the showrooms.

Of course, these were the early days of racing. Nowadays, stock cars may look at first glance like the cars coming out of the manufacturers' lots, but underneath the bodies, the cars are anything but "stock." In fact, due largely to safety reasons, the cars have changed considerably over the years. If you have the chance to see a stock car up close, you'll notice the roll cages and window nets to protect the driver, a hose-like feature that filters fresh air into the car, and flaps on top of the car for deflecting air during dangerous spins. You'll also notice that the cars have no headlights or brake lights. We all know the cars can go very fast, but there's no

FUN FACT

It could cost up to $300 million dollars to race a Formula One car for a season, compared to roughly $10 million in CART and $7-8 million in NASCAR.

FUN FACT

NASCAR Winston Cup cars have 22-gallon fuel tanks. Drivers do not have a fuel gauge, but instead rely on a fuel pressure gauge that fluctuates as fuel runs low.

speedometer in the car to actually tell the drivers how fast they are going.

These stock cars are made completely from scratch - every one of them. And, the cars are so complex that it takes about 80 days just to build one. That's a long way off from assembly-line work. Could you imagine General Motors taking 80 days to build one car?

While these cars are certainly expensive and time consuming to build, it pales in comparison to the amount of money necessary to race a Grand Prix (Formula One) or Indy Car. In an attempt to maintain some parity, and to allow a broader population the chance to compete, NASCAR has refused to use some of the sophisticated technology that the open-wheel series use. In open-wheel racing, if you don't have unlimited funds for significant amounts of highly technical research and the latest computer technology, you're at a major disadvantage.

This is not to say that all stock car teams are equal. Some are funded much better than others (particularly the multi-car teams). So, don't plan on raiding your piggy bank to buy a stock car and go win the next race. Aside from the obvious reasons why you can't just jump in a car and win, the cars, engines and teams have become highly sophisticated over the years.

STOCK CAR BASICS...

- The cars use carburetors, not fuel-injection systems (which are used in almost every street car made today).
- The cars all run on the same fuel: 108 octane gasoline. Unocal gasoline is provided free of charge.
- Cars have to weigh at least 3,400 pounds with a driver allowance of 200 pounds. In fact, the driver's side of the car cannot weigh more than 1600 pounds. If a driver weighs 200 pounds, he won't have to add any more weight to the car. But if he or she weighs less than 200 lbs, extra lead weights must be added to the car to balance things out. In fact, NASCAR requires almost everything on the car to be standardized.
- Tires are regulated by NASCAR. In fact, tires are the only part of the car that is absolutely the same on every car. Every team uses Goodyear tires because in 1997, Goodyear signed a deal and became NASCAR's exclusive supplier.
- Aerodynamic flow (how a car cuts through the air to gain more speed) is very important in racing which is why teams spend a significant amount of time perfecting the design of the car to make the aerodynamics more efficient.

• Suspension is important when handling a car at top speeds. A race team will adjust the suspension through a variety of means including changing spring pressures, tire pressures and shocks.

THE HORSEPOWER HAS IT...

Picture sitting at a stoplight, looking over at the car lined up next to you, revving your engines, just waiting to see who can accelerate and speed through the light first. You're feeling pretty cool. But, consider that in auto racing, cars have more than three times the amount of horsepower your car has. And the teams constantly work on the engines to churn out every extra little bit of horsepower. In fact, the engine is the one area of the car that is really nothing like a regular passenger car.

Every team is very secretive about what type of modifications they're making on the engines. Of course, if you read the NASCAR rulebook, you'd be overwhelmed with the minute details specifying the location of the engine in the car, the size of the engine, the parts used, etc. In fact, even though these engines have far more horsepower than most people imagine, the rules do try to require that as many parts as possible be "stock."

HELPFUL HINT

A team will often use two different engines in one car during one event. For the qualifying rounds, a team will use an engine that is built for pure speed in quick bursts. In the race itself, teams will use more sturdy engines.

TRACK TALK...

Each different kind of track requires different cars and different strategies.

Super Speedways

These are tracks that are one or more miles around. Currently, two of the super-speedways on the Winston Cup schedule - Daytona International Speedway (2.5 miles) and Talladega Superspeedway (2.66 miles) - require restrictor plates. Due to the length of these tracks and the steep banking in the turns, speeds can get too fast to ensure the safety of drivers and fans. Therefore, NASCAR regulates the speeds by using restrictor plates in the cars. Restrictor plates function as you would expect a "restrictor" to function - as a way to prevent, or restrict, extremely high speeds on superspeedways by limiting the engine rotations to 6,500 to 7,000 RPMs versus 9,000 for an open engine. Top speeds at these tracks top out at 200-202 mph. If these tracks didn't require restrictor plates, cars could run up to 240 mph, which would make insurance companies very unhappy.

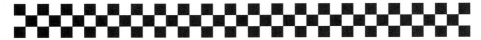

HELPFUL HINT

Because restrictor plates are used on the biggest superspeedways, drivers need another way to make their cars go faster. That is where drafting comes in. Picture two cars, one right in front of the other. The second car tails the first and, by doing so, avoids the air resistance that the first car encounters. This helps the second car go faster with less engine effort (less air resistance). Why would the first car allow the second car to draft? The beauty of drafting is that it also helps the first car go faster.

FUN FACT

The first person to drive a stock car over 200 mph was Elzie Wylie (Buddy) Baker during a tire test at Talladega in 1970.

If a superspeedway does not require restrictor plates, then drivers rely on grooves. The groove describes the fastest line around the track. There can be one- or two-groove tracks (meaning there can be one fast line or two fast lines around the track).

As you can deduce, if there are two fast lines (a high line and a low line) around the track, drivers find it eas-

Drafting actually makes both cars go faster.

ier to pass other cars. But, if there's only one fast line around a track, pit stops become an important way for a car to gain better positioning on the track. Average laps on these superspeedways are pretty consistent at 180-185 mph. Top speeds are generally in the 195-199 mph range, occasionally topping 200 mph.

Since a NASCAR driver spends most of his career racing counter-clockwise around oval-shaped tracks, his racing is comprised primarily of left turns. Exceptions are road racing courses, which are irregularly shaped.

HELPFUL HINT

If the Watkins Glen or Sears Point race is coming up and you hear talk of a team being the favorite to win, say, "Yes, that team's got a chance, if the driver remembers how to turn right."

Short Tracks

These tracks are less than one mile in length. One lap around these tracks can take as little as 15 seconds, so you'll see many more cars being lapped on one of these tracks. Just think, if a pit stop (which on average takes between 16-20 seconds) falters and takes 30 seconds, your car can lose an extra lap.

Road Courses

Road courses require drivers to master straightaways as well as left- and right-hand turns. Road-racing skills are different from the skills used in oval-track racing. The only two road courses in Winston Cup racing are Sears Point and Watkins Glen.

As you've seen, NASCAR rules are pretty stringent. How can they possibly enforce all these rules and restrictions? Actually, they do a pretty good job. NASCAR officials inspect every car before each race. And if that isn't enough, the top three finishers need to

FUN FACT

Competition is intense in racing. For example, Jack Roush received a letter alerting him that his competitor (whom he assumed was Jeff Gordon) had used an illegal substance on his tires during a race. The media got wind of a possible infraction and all eyes were on Gordon.

After an inspection of the tires, NASCAR declared that no substance was found, and Gordon was cleared of all charges.

NOT SO FUN FACT

NASCAR became highly concerned about excessive speeds when Bobby Allison crashed into a fence in front of the grandstands at Talladega and almost took out a group of fans watching the race.

FUN FACT

Goodyear supplies all the tires for the cars. At a cost of $1300 for a set, the bill for one car's weekend race could be as high as $15,600 just for tires.

offer up their cars for another routine inspection after the race, just in case something wasn't caught before the event.

A pit crew will often change the tires on only one side of the car during a pit stop because the "outside" tires wear much faster. And they do it in seconds!

Thoughts on Racing

Crew Chief Bill Ingle

The crew chief is responsible for managing the team, called the crew which prepares and services the car, and supports the driver driving the race. Bill Ingle, former crew chief for Ricky Rudd shares some thoughts on life in the NASCAR fast lane.

On the difference between being a crew chief and being a coach

Hands down, being a NASCAR crew chief is more difficult because we don't pay our crews enough to demand of them what stick-and-ball sports do. With our guys, you feel guilty - especially with the weekend guys.

On the importance of teamwork

The driver is 75% of the outcome of the race. The other 25% is the car and the team (engine, tires and aerodynamics). What's so great, though, is the driver is the first to thank the rest of the crew (the team) because he knows that he raced well due to the preparation and commitment from his team members.

How has racing changed over the years?

It was more fun back in the early days. It was more of a laid-back atmosphere, and we all joined up and wanted to be involved because it was plain fun. In the old days, there were no specialists ... everyone just worked on the cars together. Also, nowadays, there are so many restrictions and rules. It takes some of the fun out of racing.

Is it possible to have a personal life with the schedule you keep?

You have to be dedicated because it's tough on your personal life. With all of the traveling and time commitments, you have to really love the sport. We work, on average, twelve- to fourteen-hour days. And the season never ends. I've had three families since I've been involved in this sport. That's not fun, so I must really love this sport. It's easier for the drivers, though. The drivers' spouses usually don't work, and the drivers can afford to bring their spouses to the races with them. If you're not a driver, and just part of the team, you usually can't afford to bring your spouse to the track every weekend.

As a crew chief, what's your biggest responsibility?

In many ways, you need to act like a parent. You need to keep morale up, which is the toughest part of the job. Of course, you also strategize, fix problems that arise at the track and in the shop and meet with fabricators and mechanics. But the biggest responsibility is the crew. When you're losing, you need to keep their morale up, and when you're winning, you need to make sure they don't start celebrating too early - before the checkered flag drops. With the drivers, you really need to parent them. One thing with a driver, if he doesn't perform well, you need to restore his confidence immediately or the whole team will be affected. The worst thing for the team is when the driver loses confidence.

What are some of the superstitions you've run across in your years of racing?

It used to be that drivers wouldn't race with $50 bills in their wallets or pockets. For some reason, they were considered unlucky.

Junior Johnson was apparently pretty superstitious. He wouldn't eat peanuts with shells. The shells made him mad. And Kyle Petty apparently had a lucky t-shirt.

LAP 5
The Flags

You're at the track and you see a bunch of colorful flags, and you hear people saying things like, "Dale Earnhardt took the checkered flag last weekend at Daytona." You know what that phrase means, but you'll need to know a bit more about the flags to really understand what's going on.

Understanding the colors of the flags in motorsports is like understanding the symbol for touchdowns and field goals in football. Here's a run down of the eight flags.

Green Flag

The green flag signals that the race has officially started. It is considered an honor to wave the green flag before a race, and major races often give that responsibility to celebrities, politicians, or other public figures.

Despite the symbolic importance of the green flag at the start of the race, the cars start running long before the drivers see the green flag. The drivers will follow a pace car for a few laps to get all 43 cars up to the same speed for the start of the race. Think about it. If the race began from a standing start and you were driving a car back in the second half of the field, by the time you got your car going at a competitive speed, the lead car would already be too far ahead of you to reasonably catch up. By allowing the pace cars to set the speed (which will also be the pit-road speed), all of the cars have the opportunity to warm up their engines and get situated on the track. When the green flag drops, the cars are lined up and ready to go racing.

HELPFUL HINT

In NASCAR, two pace cars lead the field.
One pace car leads the first half of the drivers (about 20), while the other pace car guides the second half of the field.

FUN FACT

Talk about getting out the vote. On March 21, 1976, at the Atlanta 500, then-Governor Jimmy Carter took time out of his busy presidential run to throw the green flag and announce to the gathered press that if he were elected President, he would invite some of the NASCAR folks over to visit the White House. After the election, he kept his promise.

Also, the green flag again appears after a caution period, signaling that the race can continue at a normal pace.

Yellow Flag

The yellow flag signals that something dangerous (e.g. an accident or debris on the track) has occurred and that drivers need to slow down. Once the caution period concludes, drivers don't just gun their engines and take off. Again, there are rules that apply. If you haven't already figured it out, NASCAR has rules and guidelines for almost everything occurring on the track. Yellow flags are fairly common in racing and may occur multiple times in a race.

At the restart, the following can occur:

1) If no car has been lapped on the track, then drivers will restart in a single-file line.

2) If a car has been lapped, then drivers restart in double file. The race leader lines up in the front row on the outside followed by the others cars on the lead lap. The lapped cars will line up on the inside.

Be sure to listen to the announcers to see which driver is leading the race, or you may look kind of silly cheering for the driver who's been lapped. However, if there are only 25 laps left in the race, go ahead and cheer. Only the cars on the lead lap get to line up in the outside lane for a restart. Just to add to the confusion, if there are fewer than 10 laps left, the cars line up in single file.

Red Flag

Did you ever play the game red light/green light? Drivers play that game on a larger scale. As you can probably guess, the red flag signals the drivers to stop. Races stop for many reasons, including bad weather or a serious accident on the track. When the red flag flies, everyone stops what they're doing - even the pit crews. The most common cause of a red flag is rain, which makes a track slick and therefore dangerous. In the event that a race is interrupted by rain, the drivers pull over in the order they are in at the time of the red flag and wait for the conditions to improve.

HELPFUL HINT

If you're just walking in to the room after a caution period, be careful not to assume that the car at the front of the outside line is the race leader. If a lapped car stays on the track during a caution when all of the leaders pit, then that driver is allowed to take the outside (lead) lap on the restart. By staying on the track, that driver actually passed all of the cars that pitted, and therefore regained the lap. That driver is likely, however, to fall behind again when he takes his (postponed) pit stop. Starting at the front with the leaders right behind is called starting at the tail end of the lead lap.

Black Flag

When a driver sees the black flag, he's not happy. While most other flags apply to all the drivers in the field, an official can black flag a single driver. All the other drivers can continue on their merry way, while the black-flagged driver must immediately pull into his pit stall. An official will black flag a driver because he sees the driver doing something wrong, or because there is something wrong with the car.

Black Flag with White Cross

If you thought the black flag was bad, the black flag with the white cross is even worse. If a driver ignores the black flag, the officials will signal him with a black flag with a white cross, which means that his laps will no longer count.

White Flag

Of course, if you have a black flag, you must have a white flag. The white flag simply signals that there is only one lap left to go in the race.

Checkered Flag

The checkered flag signals the winner at the end of the race.

A yellow flag can mean a lot of things, but it almost always means trouble.

From Football to NASCAR

JOE GIBBS

Joe Gibbs - yes, the same Joe Gibbs that coached the Washington Redskins to a Super Bowl championship, is the owner and manager of one of NASCAR's premier racing teams. In fact, he has another place in history as the only person to have coached a winning Super Bowl team and a winning race team in the Daytona 500. Joe Gibbs Racing has been the beneficiary of the superb driving of Bobby Labonte for the last few years, and now also includes former Indy Racing League Champion Tony Stewart.

Joe briefly explains how he became such a big fan of racing and reflects on the differences and similarities between being a football coach and the owner of a race team.

Joe Gibbs

BB: Are there any fundamental principles that you have applied to running both a successful football team and race team? If so, what are they?

JG: Both sports require you to be in the "people business." It is a matter of picking the right people for each job or position. In both sports, each position is specialized, and it is a must to have the most qualified person in that job. You do not win with "Xs" and "Os" and you do not win with cars. You win with people.

BB: How did you become such a big race fan? Did you follow racing your whole life?

JG: In high school in the 50s, I got hooked on street rods and have had a love of cars and racing ever since. It just seemed like a natural progression for me to go into racing when I got out of football.

BB: Which is more stressful? Being a Winston Cup crew chief or an NFL coach?

JG: Each of these has a high degree of stress involved. I would probably say that, on a day-to-day basis, a Winston Cup crew chief and an NFL coach experience more diverse levels of stress than most people realize.

BB: Which requires a higher level of strategic thinking, NASCAR pit strategy or NFL play strategy?

JG: I would say they are the same. It takes guts to make the tough calls in both sports.

BB: Which one is a more grueling season, a Winston Cup 34-race season or an NFL 16-game regular season?

JG: A Winston Cup season. These guys have a grueling schedule. This is a tough job and requires enormous commitment from them. I have great appreciation and respect for their wives and families who are so supportive during the race season.

LAP 6
NASCAR Memorable Moments

It's always difficult to name the most memorable moments in sports. It's pretty subjective most of the time, because what's memorable to some may not be memorable to others. If you're a novice to NASCAR, however, there are a few races that are must-knows, and some that are just plain interesting. These races are often cited as some of the most memorable. You'll be considered a true racing fan if you remember these classic racing stories.

The 1976 Daytona 500 (The Rivalry)

Even if you don't recall any other race, this one is the most important, most entertaining, and most talked about race in the history of NASCAR.

What made this race amazing were all the events leading up to the big day. This race featured one of the greatest rivalries in all of motorsports — Richard Petty and David Pearson — at perhaps the greatest, most anticipated event on the circuit, the Daytona 500. In itself, this would be enough to make a memorable race, but the 1976 Daytona 500 included a number of "dirty" incidents during Speedweek and, of course, a crash or two.

The top three drivers in the qualifying rounds were disqualified because of illegal enhancements (in two of the cases, using laughing gas) to increase the speed of their cars. After causing a huge commotion and demanding to be allowed back in the running, A.J. Foyt, Darrell Waltrip and Dave Marcis, managed to convince the NASCAR folks to allow them to re-qualify, which they all did.

As the race got underway, fans immediately felt the tension between Pearson and Petty. Neck and neck for most of the race, the real excitement came on the last lap. Pearson masterfully drafted behind Petty before the white flag signaled the last and final lap of the race. The aerodynamic boost of drafting helped Pearson slightly edge Petty out of the first turn ... at least until the next turn, where Petty barely slid ahead. But that's where the excitement came in.

FUN FACT

You hear of fake plays in football (play-action passes for instance), but were you aware that you can fake out an opponent in racing as well? Again, with the Pearson-Petty rivalry, NASCAR saw one of the greatest trick plays. David Pearson pretended to have engine failure on the final lap of the Firecracker 400 at Daytona in 1974, causing Richard Petty to pass him. As Petty drove past, Pearson quickly geared up and shot past Petty to win the race.

Coming out of the last turn, Petty slid straight into the wall and skidded into the infield where his engine completely died. Pearson hit the wall as well, but was able to maneuver his car well enough to limp across the finish line and win the race. While Richard Petty sat in his car in the grassy infield just feet away from the finish line, his crew pushed the car over to Pearson's, where a fist-fight promptly ensued.

HELPFUL HINT

Nitrous oxide, better known as laughing gas, is not just used in the dentist's office. It has been used illegally by some drivers to increase the performance of their cars.

The 1979 Daytona 500 (The Fight)

Talking about great races doesn't necessarily mean just the close finishes or the intense rivalries. It also means the most talked about...for whatever reason people talk. The 1979 Daytona 500 certainly goes down as one of the most talked about.

First, let's set the scene. The race took place on a particularly stormy day for most of the nation. Sports fans had nothing to do but stay inside and watch TV. For the first time in NASCAR history, a network (CBS) telecast the entire 500-

mile race from start to finish. As sports fans across the country tuned into an exciting and drama-filled afternoon, CBS saw its ratings soar. As it turned out, this race put NASCAR on the map.

For most of the day, fans saw a pretty competitive afternoon of racing. Cale Yarborough and Donnie Allison bumped a few times, but remained on each other's tails for most of the race. On the last lap, Yarborough and Allison (Donnie) hit so hard that they each went spinning into the infield, unable to finish the race. What happened next really makes this event memorable.

With testosterone abounding, Cale and Donnie got out of their cars with the (supposed) intention of "talking." Then, Bobby Allison (Donnie's brother) saw the two arguing, finished the race and drove over to where the two drivers were. There's a dispute as to what was said and who started the aggression, but the next thing the CBS national audience saw was Bobby jumping out of his car and pummeling Cale.

HELPFUL HINT

When a driver fails to qualify for a race, he must leave the track. This guideline is now called the "Darrell Waltrip Rule." In 1975 at the Motor State 400, Darrell Waltrip failed to qualify and, refusing to take no for an answer, decided to pay a group of alternates for their spots, until he found a ride in a car that had qualified.

The 1998 Daytona 500
(The Monkey off his Back)

Two proverbial monkeys were shown the door in the world of professional sports during 1998. John Elway,

FUN FACT

Bill Elliott set the fastest qualifying lap at Daytona with a speed of 210.364 mph. He also holds the fastest and second-fastest all-time qualifying laps in the history of the NASCAR Winston Cup Series at 212.809 and 212.229.

FUN FACT

January 31, 1960, CBS became the first network to air a NASCAR special covering the qualifying rounds for the Daytona 500.

FUN FACT

When Darrell Waltrip won the Daytona 500 in 1989, he broke out into a post-race celebratory "Ickey Shuffle" modeled after the former flamboyant Cincinnati Bengals football player, Ickey Woods.

FUN FACT

Bobby Allison had a pretty cool 1983. He not only won his first and only Winston Cup Championship, but was also invited along with his wife, Judy, to dine with President Ronald and Nancy Reagan at the White House.

quarterback of football's Denver Broncos, finally won a Super Bowl, and Dale Earnhardt finally won his Super Bowl - the Daytona 500. Dale Earnhardt, seven-time winner of the prestigious Winston Cup and one of the best stock car drivers in history, had never won NASCAR's most important race in twenty years of trying. Even a fair-weather fan will remember the emotional ending to this race.

Earnhardt's car ran well all day, but it wasn't until the final 23 laps that the real drama began. Earnhardt's teammate, Mike Skinner, sidled up to Earnhardt's car after the green flag came out following the second caution period. Skinner gave Earnhardt an important aerodynamic boost to push his car out front, and that made the difference. Earnhardt kept a comfortable lead and won the race.

FUN FACT

Father-Son Dynamic Duo... In 1993, Dale Jarrett won his very first Daytona 500 while his father, Ned Jarrett, calling the race for CBS, cheered him on.

As a fan, the most memorable part of this race was the aftermath. Seeing the other teams' crew members lined up on pit road to "high five" and congratulate Earnhardt turned the race from an individual triumph to a spectacular outpouring of warmth by the entire sport. And then, to top it off, Earnhardt demonstrated his showmanship by carving a number 3 (his car number) on the infield grass before driving into victory lane.

Darlington Raceway, 1950 (The Beginning of a new Era)

Before 1950, stock cars raced on dirt tracks. In fact, the thought of having a stock car race on anything but a dirt track seemed ridiculous. At the time, the only cars racing on non-dirt tracks were the foreign made cars racing in the Indy 500. Harold Brasington took in an Indy race and became so enamored with the track, he wanted to build something similar in Darlington, South Carolina.

FUN FACT

In 1969, fans could see the Daytona 500 for as little as $6 for an infield seat. Reserved seats today go for $75-90.

Race fans now consider Harold a visionary, but at the time, even the most passionate race fans thought he was crazy. Nevertheless, Harold made racing history by building an egg-shaped track that is now considered one of the most difficult tracks on the circuit.

With no pre-sales, Harold had no idea how many people would attend the inaugural race on Labor Day 1950. He assumed, at best, 5,000 people might come to check it out. In his wildest dreams, he could not have foreseen the onslaught of 25,000 people appearing at the track the morning of the race. Of course he was thrilled, but he had only built bleachers to hold 9,000 people. So he resorted to selling tickets to the infield of the track, beginning a popular racing custom which continues today.

The race turned out to be a huge success, and The Southern 500 (as it was named) is now a Labor Day institution. And, even more significant, the success at Darlington paved the way for building other superspeedways. By the way, a driver by the name of Johnny Mantz won this 500-mile race by driving at an average speed of only 76 mph. (Racing was a little different back then...)

HELPFUL HINT

When referring to Darlington Raceway, feel free to say "The Lady in Black." You'll really look like you know what you're talking about.

The 1985 Southern 500 at Darlington (The Million)

In 1985, to add a little more excitement to the sport of racing, R.J. Reynolds offered a bonus of $1 million to any driver who could win three of four specific Winston Cup races in one season. The four races included the Daytona 500 (the most prestigious), the Winston 500 at Talladega (the fastest), the Coca-Cola 600 (the longest), and the Darlington Southern 500 (the oldest). Bill Elliott took the racing world by surprise and, at the Southern 500, ran a spectacular race to win the million-dollar prize called the Winston Million.

The fact that Bill Elliott won this award in its first year offered was pretty amazing when you consider that it took twelve years for another driver to repeat the same feat. Gaining less attention, but certainly worth noting, was that the 1985 Southern 500 marked the last race at this track for the legendary David Pearson.

FUN FACT

From the 1930s to the 1950s, races started based on the ebb and flow of the tides.

Nothing beats winning!

LAP 7

Interview with

Andy Papa

Pit Crew Coach

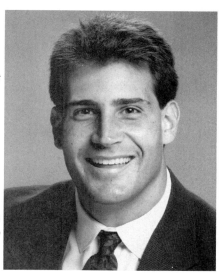

Andy Papathanassiou

Given the big dollars involved in NASCAR, it makes sense that teams have developed systems to shave valuable seconds off of pit stops. A NASCAR team in top form can change four tires and add 22 gallons of fuel in less than 20 seconds. A botched pit stop can cost a driver valuable seconds or hundreds of yards.

Much of the innovation in pit stop procedure has come from the evolution of the position of pit crew coach, and much of this evolution can be attributed to the man who originated the position and has made it commonplace on the best race teams.

Andy Papathanassiou (pronounced, papa-thana-see-you) is the man who started it all. Andy Papa (as he likes to be called) is the pit crew coach for the Hendrick Motorsports DuPont-sponsored Winston Cup team. Simply put, he coaches the pit crew of Jeff Gordon's #24 team that won the 1995, 1997 and 1998 NASCAR Winston Cup championships.

Andy may not be a household name like Jeff Gordon - yet. But he's created such a unique and important position on the team, other race teams constantly try to duplicate his coaching style and techniques.

Every second lost during a pit stop could mean hundreds of thousands of dollars in winnings for a team. So, as you can imagine, trying to coordinate the efforts of a seven-person crew that performs pit stops is a huge undertaking. Andy Papa has thrived in this environment and has been vital to the continued success of the #24 DuPont team, known as the "Rainbow Warriors."

BB: How did you become so committed to racing? Is it something you grew up with?

AP: I grew up with an interest in cars, but I never figured I would do anything with it. I was always very athletic, though. In high school (in New Jersey) I lettered in football, wrestling and track, and was voted a USA Today All-American. I was recruited by Stanford University and given a football scholarship. I also was on the track team and played rugby for Stanford. After graduation, I jumped on the chance to represent Stanford and play rugby in Australia. I also traveled to Greece, where my relatives live. So, how does this relate to racing? Well, when I returned to California, I went in for back surgery. I had a ruptured disk from all the abuses I endured playing sports.

While I was flat on my back recovering from surgery, I made a list of all the things I wanted to explore. Racing was on the list. I always had an interest in cars, but

never had the chance to follow up. Of course, at the time, I still needed a job. I was hired at Oracle Software Corporation, although I was never fully satisfied there. A short time later, in 1991, I noticed that the NASCAR circuit was coming to Sonoma County near San Francisco. I figured I would go check it out and see what might happen.

On the first day of practice, I got there at 6:00 a.m. I knew that I had to look non-touristy to fit in, so I wore blue jeans, a work-type shirt and a red windbreaker - which turned out to be significant.

The crews started showing up in the garage area at about 7:00 a.m. One of the crews was wearing red team jackets. Bingo. I fell in right behind them and maneuvered my way in. I even went so far as to pretend to have a conversation with the guys as we were walking in. Of course, I was really only speaking to myself, but no one said anything. All the teams unload their cars behind their haulers, so I just went down the line of haulers asking the teams if they needed help.

One of the first guys I came across was Buddy Parrott (well-known crew chief/team manager, currently with the #99 car). At the time, Buddy was the crew chief for the #10 Purolator racing team. He seemed interested in getting some extra help and asked if I had credentials. Of course, I said yes (even though I didn't), and I went to work sweeping the garage area, cleaning up the car and running for tires. By race time, Buddy even let me wear his spare uniform and increased my duties from sweeping to running gas cans.

Knowing that this race was on national TV made me realize there were many more opportunities out there. I asked Buddy what he thought would be the next step - how I could really get involved. The first thing I was told to do was move to Charlotte, North Carolina. So, two months later, I gave notice at my job and headed to Charlotte. I started off continuing to work for Buddy's team, even though Buddy was no longer there.

BB: Is that where you started working as a pit crew coordinator?

AP: No. I pretty much did odd jobs to really learn the business. Eventually, I realized that since I had the athletic background, I should see if I could help out athletically. I would set aside time for all of us pit crew guys to practice. At the time, I was working as a jack man, meaning I jacked the car up so we could change tires on pit stops. As a result of our practice sessions, our pit-stop times definitely improved.

BB: Were other teams practicing pit stops then?

AP: No, most teams really didn't dedicate time to practicing pit stops. Racing evolved from a time when each team member "did it all," into a sport with very specialized positions like chassis mechanics, fabricators, aerodynamics and motor specialists. Pit crews are just now starting to benefit from the same kind of specialization. Because our pit crew doesn't work on the car, they can devote more time to pit stops.

BB: How did you get involved with Ray Evernham and Hendrick Motorsports?

AP: There's always turnover in teams, and when new crew chiefs come in they tend to bring in their own guys. A crew chief change on the #10 car caused just such a change, and I was released from my job there. But, as luck would have it, Alan Kulwicki's team was looking for a new jack man. I had a tryout and was hired. I was there almost a full season when, through a mutual friend, I met Ray Evernham. Ray was looking for someone to do what I wanted to do with the pit crews. So, in August of 1992, I started working with Ray as a jack man and trainer for the pit crew.

BB: Since pit crews were not accustomed to training, what kind of workouts did you have in the beginning?

AP: We didn't have any equipment, so I had to use my imagination to make due. In fact, I used certain drills that I picked up while traveling to Australia in my rugby days. We would use our body weight as much as possible. We used anything in the shop to help us, such as 70-pound tires and 25-pound jack stands. Sometimes I'd make the guys carry each other on their backs and run around the parking lot. We'd also improvise with wheelbarrow races for strength and coordination.

BB: What do you do differently now?

AP: We have a 2,600 square foot weight room and locker room now, so it makes the workouts much easier. In fact, most of the new shops now have weight rooms.

> A workout today might look something like this:
>
> Two practice sessions a week for 1-1/2 to 2 hours, and a team meeting once a week to talk about where we need to improve
>
> Lifting weights 2-3 times per week
>
> Stretching
>
> Practice drills to improve timing on pit stops
>
> As for diet, we generally understand good eating habits but we don't enforce anything

Life "in the pits" can mean long hours of tedium punctuated by moments of intense action.

BB: When you're taking notes during a race, what kind of things are you jotting down?

AP: When Jeff would talk to Ray and describe the handling of the car, Ray would then decide what adjustments needed to be made during pit stops. I write down everything Jeff says and what lap he said it on. This serves as a record leading up to any car adjustments, and it gives us a heads-up on what those adjustments might be. I also have a form where I list all the information about the stop, like what lap we came in on, whether it was a caution or green-flag stop, two or four tires, how many gallons of gas and what kind of adjustments, if any, we made.

At a recent race at Rockingham, N.C., here's some of what I wrote:

> Lap #38 - tight in the middle (of the corner)
>
> Lap #61 - pushing hard
>
> Lap #80 - green flag pit stop, changed four tires, filled 18 gallons of gas, one round (of adjustment) in rear to take out tightness

BB: Being a coach, what kind of motivational tactics do you use?

AP: I have to put myself in the shoes of the people I'm training, so I try to instill confidence in them that we can do this job better than any other team. Even though pit stops are fast, if we rush through it we will make mistakes and produce a slow stop. We must believe in our technique and our ability in order to really do well. Before a race, we'll have a brief meeting, and then break on a certain word. Each race is different. Sometimes we'll break on "Win" or "Consistency" or even just silence - which is always kind of a crowd favorite. Whatever the word is, it's the theme for the day.

To be honest, I don't need to work hard at getting the team motivated. We're all professionals who love the sport, and everyone is aware of how they fit into the team and how important their individual jobs are to the whole effort. We never make excuses for problems. Everyone here is treated as an adult. If you can't make practice, you communicate beforehand. After a race, we don't get down on ourselves if we make mistakes. We practice to eliminate any recurring mistakes. We don't ever want to let the team down. We want to help the team win races. We even dress nicely when we go to a race because it's important to feel professional.

BB: Since you used to play football and were an integral part of the team, how would you characterize the difference and similarities between being part of a NASCAR pit crew and being part of a football team?

AP: As far as teamwork, NASCAR and football have similarities. In football, you have eleven people on the field at one time. If there's a breakdown in one of the positions, then the play won't work. On a NASCAR pit stop, the stopwatch records the slowest person, so if six people do everything perfectly and the seventh person is slow, the stopwatch for that particular pit stop will record a slower time for the team as a whole.

On the other hand, the teamwork aspect of the two sports also has some differences. In NASCAR we don't compete against another person - there's no defense. With football, it's a zero-sum game, meaning one team wins, one team losses. In NASCAR, we don't compare ourselves to others. We just have to do our best, regardless of what other teams are doing. If our system is superior and if we focus our ability in order to execute it well, then we will be victorious.

Training is different as well. Pit crew training is not as strength intensive as in football. We try to increase our fitness and endurance levels. In football, the workout is geared toward strength and explosive movements. In NASCAR racing, since we are the guys that set up before the race and tear everything down after the race, our explosive 16-second pit stops are done within the context of a four-hour race within a twenty-hour work day. For that reason, we concentrate more on muscular endurance and injury prevention.

BB: You mentioned that the pit crew flies in the morning of the race. Isn't that a little risky? What if the plane gets delayed?

AP: Well, we've actually been in that situation. Two years ago at the Talladega race, we tried to fly in that morning. There were thunderstorms preventing us from landing, so we flew to Birmingham, 60 miles away. As we landed in Birmingham the weather cleared up and the track started to dry. Most of the pit crews weren't at the track because, like us, they couldn't land in Talladega.

We started driving to the track while listening to the announcers on the radio preparing for the start of the race. The crews at the track were scrambling to fill their pit crew rosters, because someone would need to pit the car until we showed up. If you had any pit experience at all, you were temporarily drafted to pit someone's car.

With only one lap to go before the cars took the green flag - with us still at least 15 minutes away - it started to rain again. By the time we made it to the gate, the race was postponed, and we had to turn around and drive back to Birmingham. The thing is, though, the race would have gone on without us.

BB: What's the pressure like during the NASCAR season?

AP: First, you have to understand that the NASCAR season is basically never over. We never have an off-season. Races take place from February through the end of November, and then December and January is spent getting ready for February.

Also, most of the pit crew guys have other jobs they have to go to during the week. So, for anyone on the team it's a seven-day-a-week job. And, for the weekend warriors (the pit crew) it's a six-day-a-week job, in addition to holding down a regular job.

As you can imagine then, the pressure is constant during the year. Sometimes it seems overwhelming, but much of the time, it's good pressure. Part of this good pressure comes from the feeling that we can win races every weekend. It's what we spend so much time preparing to do.

Yet, even if you finish the season having won the Winston Cup championship, you still will have lost more races than you've won over the course of the year. So, when you win, it's often a relief, because sometimes you are prepared to win and circumstances dictate otherwise. Sure, you celebrate and appreciate each win, but the celebration doesn't last long because the next day you're back in the shop preparing for the following weekend.

Even with all of this pressure, the grueling hours and the limited time with your family, every one of us feels blessed to be part of the excitement. We wouldn't trade it for the world.

LAP 8
The Point System
THE ROAD TO THE WINSTON CUP CHAMPIONSHIP

Back in the early days of stock car racing, any driver who won a race could claim he was the best in the sport. When racing incorporated, Big Bill France instituted a point system to ensure that there would be a recognized and undisputed champion.

The point system was also designed to reward maximum participation and effort by drivers throughout the season. Not all sports can make this claim. A top tennis player may skip minor tournaments to rest up for a grand slam event. But NASCAR rewards persistence and durability as well as speed. Only under dire circumstances will a driver miss a race. And, we're talking about every race on the NASCAR Winston Cup circuit, not just the most recognizable or popular ones. The point system awards points to any driver that starts a race. The key is that a driver must enter and qualify for the race to get even the minimum number of points.

First place = 175 points

Second place = 170 points

Third place = 165 points

Fourth place = 160 points

Fifth place = 155 points

Sixth place = 150 points

Seventh place = 146 points

Eighth-eleventh places are separated by four points.

Three points separate every position from eleventh to 43rd place.

At the end of the year, NASCAR officials add up the points and the driver with the most points wins. A driver isn't in this alone, however. The car owner benefits as well. Car owners also receive points when their cars enter races.

You don't need an advanced degree in mathematics or statistics to figure out the system ... it's pretty simple.

Just like earning extra credit in school, drivers can earn extra points throughout a race.

The Front Runner

Drivers have an incentive to take the lead during a race because a driver will earn five extra points for leading at the end of at least one lap. Therefore, the winner of a race earns a minimum of 180 points: 175 points for finishing in first place, plus five bonus points for leading the last lap.

HELPFUL HINT

Even if a driver is replaced midway through the race by another driver, the driver who starts the race will earn all the points.

FUN FACT

Terry Labonte won the Winston Cup title in 1996 with points, but only won two races while Jeff Gordon won 10 races and came in second in points.

Points for Car Owners

Car owners receive points when their cars (regardless of who's driving them) enter races. Why is it important for car owners to win points, you ask? First, they win a championship at the end of the season, just like the drivers do. Also, these car owner points help determine starting positions when weather disrupts qualifying rounds, or when ties occur during qualifying.

HELPFUL HINT

A driver cannot earn five points every time he circles the track. The five-point bonus is only awarded to a driver once during a race. If this were not the case, then imagine what would happen... If Mark Martin wins the Daytona 500 (200 laps) and leads every lap, then he would earn 1175 points [175 points + (5 x 200)].

Even though a driver can only earn five points for leading a race, he can earn another five-point bonus for leading the most laps during a race. Therefore, the winner of the race has the ability to earn a total of 185 points.

Car owners earn points even if their drivers don't qualify for a race. They earn points based on how their cars finished in qualifying, even if they didn't make the starting lineup.

Some fans complain that the current point system rewards drivers that fail to win races. Only five points separate the top finishers in a race, so a driver can win the Winston Cup title and not win a significant number of races.

FUN FACT

In many families, NASCAR racing seems to run in the blood. Witness Brett, Geoff, and Todd Bodine, Dale Earnhardt Senior and Junior, or Bobby and Terry Labonte. In fact, in racing it is not unusual to see drivers competing against brothers or even fathers or sons. Perhaps the most famous racing families of all time are the Allisons and the Petty's, winners of twelve Daytona 500s among them.

FUN FACT

The success of top NASCAR racers often comes in streaks. For example, Cale Yarborough won the Winston Cup in 1976, 1977, and 1978. He also came in second in 1974 and 1980. Yarborough won 83 Winston Cup races in his long career.

FUN FACT

The top drivers in the 1999 NASCAR Winston Cup season were: Dale Jarret with 5,262 points and 4 race victories, Bobby Labonte with 5, 061 points and 5 victories, Mark Martin with 4,943 points and 2 wins, Tony Stewart with 4,774 points and 3 wins, Jeff Burton with 4,733 points and 6 wins and Jeff Gordon with 4,620 and 7 wins.

Jeff Gordon, one of racing's most popular figures.

From Small Town to Big Time

Pit Crew Member Tony Ederle

BB: How is it that being from a really small town of only 4000 people, you became such a big fan of racing?

TE: I was born in Chassee, Missouri, a town of about 4000 people. I used to be a drag racer and worked on a bunch of friends' cars when I was little. In fact, I started working on cars when I was five years old. When they built a circle track within 15-30 minutes of town, I began to race dirt tracks every weekend. I lived on a farm, so I was always mechanically inclined. I knew everything about cars, although I have to admit I'm still learning new things every day.

I really started my NASCAR career five years ago when I moved to North Carolina. I wasn't making any money in Missouri, so I just decided to leave. It's a tough state to make money in racing.

I started as a jack man, working for a bunch of different people. I worked for Jeremy Mayfield and Cale Yarborough, then after a while, I went back to Missouri. When I arrived back home, I heard about another job and turned right around the

As often as not, races are won "in the pits".

next day and drove back to North Carolina to work for Harry Ranier, who was starting a new NASCAR Busch Series team.

BB: With most teams located in or near Charlotte, is there much gossip from team to team?

TE: Everyone is always talking about who's getting fired and who's moving to what team? It's called "Silly Season," where everyone talks about who's in and who's out.

BB: What's your job now? Is there any job security?

TE: I work as a fabricator now and I have the opportunity to help the crew chief do chassis setups. I love where I am now, but there's really no job security. Everyone shops around looking for the team that will offer the most money.

BB: What's your week like?

TE: *Monday morning:* We come in early and pull the motor out of the car that raced on Sunday. If the car was wrecked, we'll send the car to the frame shop after we pull the motor out.

Tuesday: We usually try to take Tuesdays off to spend with family or friends. Sometimes we're able to take the day off, and sometimes we'll just work to make the rest of the week easier. For those guys with families, it's a much-needed day off to spend with them.

Wednesday: By 8:00 a.m. we're all at the shop. If we didn't come in on Tuesday, Wednesday could turn into a really long day. Sometimes we'll stay at the shop until 10:00 p.m., or even all night to fix the cars and get ready for the next race.

Some of what we do in the shop is make sure the car is specifically ready for the upcoming track. We'll also hook the car up to a computer to gauge the horsepower and to see how to get better performance.

Thursday: Again, we'll be there no later than 8:00 a.m. (unless we've spent the night at the shop the night before). We put the cars on the trucks and try to get the truck driver out of the garage by noon. Once the truck is gone, we'll have other miscellaneous work to do for the rest of the day. If the race is far away, like Las Vegas, the truck driver will leave by Tuesday afternoon so he can get there by Thursday evening.

Friday: We're all at the track (except the "weekend warriors" who don't need to be there until Sunday morning) by 6:00 or 7:00 a.m. to set up. We'll unload the equipment, practice, and then go out and qualify.

Friday night: The team eats together ... nothing fancy, but we'll sit around and debrief on practice and qualifying sessions. We'll definitely go to bed early because it's still a long weekend ahead.

Saturday morning: By 6:00 a.m. we're back at the track. We'll either practice during the day, or if necessary, race for a second-round qualifying spot. Then, of course, there's "Happy Hour," which is the last practice session of the day.

Saturday night: By Saturday night, we're all pretty tired, so we hang out in the hotel room, order room service or go out for a quick bite. We have a $25 a day food allowance for breakfast and dinner. We eat lunch at the track from the food in the team's trailer.

Sunday: We'll get to the track early and get ready to race. After the race, we fly or drive home and get ready to start the process all over again. If we've won the race, we'll have a little celebratory dinner with the team, but we never celebrate too long because we need to get ready to race at the next track the following weekend.

BB: Your schedules are so hectic. Are any of the guys health or fitness conscious? Do they work out or try to eat well?

TE: We all usually work out and go to the gym on our own. Everyone on the team is pretty athletic. Even at the tracks on the weekends, we'll try to find a gym to work out in. We're all pretty good at eating healthy when we're home, but at the track, it's difficult to know what you're going to get. We just eat whatever is in the trailer. Our truck driver has $150 to spend on food for us per weekend, and he usually buys lots of ham sandwiches, chips and snacks, and things that are easy to eat while we're on the go.

BB: Sounds like you spend almost every waking hour with your team. Do you ever get tired of each other?

TE: Not at all. It sounds corny, but we're all like family. You live with these guys every day and see them more than anyone else in your life. You eat with them, ride to work with them, so you just learn to get along and treat each other well.

BB: Do you ever get burnt out and wish you were doing something else?

TE: Sometimes I'll get tired or maybe bored with a track that I've been to a bunch of times, but I never really get burnt out. The race day adrenaline always kicks in and keeps me going. I think most of us feel that we're really fortunate to be doing what we're doing, so burnout never really happens.

LAP 9
Race Weekend NASCAR

Now that you know everything you need to know to enjoy a day at the races, let's look at what goes on there for the driver and his crew.

Most professional sports teams have home games and away games, and they plan accordingly. Obviously, teams prefer home games not only for the ease of travel, but also for the benefit of having a "home field advantage" (being familiar with your surroundings and having the hometown fans rooting for you). With NASCAR, there's no such thing as home field advantage and, for the most part, preparation for race weekends remains fairly consistent weekend to weekend.

The season runs almost year-round, keeping the drivers and their team members constantly busy. Hopefully, you're starting to appreciate the time commitments, preparation and camaraderie of the drivers and their crews. But race day is another world altogether. I encourage anyone who is not already a race fan to check out a race weekend, even if it's only a race on your local dirt track. You can feel the excitement and exhilaration in the air, but to give you an even better appreciation of the sport, you need to know what all those people scurrying around are doing, beginning early Friday morning.

Early Friday morning

Early Friday (about 5:00 or 6:00 in the morning), fans will see the truck drivers hauling huge pieces of equipment to the tracks. Truck drivers for teams high in the point standings get the benefit of preferred locations in the garage area. With the heavy and bulky equipment that they need to load and unload, this benefit makes the truck drivers and crews very happy.

HELPFUL HINT

NASCAR officials continually inspect the cars during race weekends... almost every time you turn around.

On Fridays, race teams have done more by mid-morning than most people will do in an entire day. These teams need to re-fit and tweak almost every inch of the race cars to make them ready for the grueling requirements of the weekend.

If you're a rookie, NASCAR requires you to go to a meeting in the morning. NASCAR doesn't mess around with rules and safety, and they absolutely want to make sure that rookies know what they're doing. If you don't need to go to the rookie meeting, then you focus on the early-morning practice session (generally before 11:00 a.m.). Then, of course, between 11:00 and the afternoon qualifying session, the car needs to go through another inspection.

FUN FACT

To demonstrate how times have changed on NASCAR weekends, just consider the types of items carried in the haulers. Some teams carry cappuccino machines with them on the road. It's hard to imagine Curtis Turner or Cale Yarborough craving double cappuccinos before races.

Qualifying

In this first qualifying round, drivers will complete a lap as fast as possible to try and make one of the first 25 positions in the starting lineup. If you've secured one of the first 25 positions, you can relax (a bit) in the afternoon - perhaps take in another practice session and then rest up for the next day.

Saturday Qualifying

If a driver fails to secure one of the top 25 spots on Friday and doesn't think his qualifying speed will be good enough to get him into the race, he needs to re-qualify on Saturday. Saturday, as you can imagine, is incredibly stressful. Only 43 teams get to race on Sunday, and if you're not one of them, your fans will be let down. Also, and just as important to the driver's future in racing, the team's sponsor will be extremely disappointed - to put it mildly. If a sponsor is spending millions of dollars to have people see their logo on a car, and fans can't see the logo because the car did not make the race, the sponsor may have second thoughts about the investment.

HELPFUL HINT

The driver with the fastest qualifying time will earn what's called the "pole." The pole winner gets to start the race on the inside of the front row. Additionally, the pole winner from every race gets to compete in the following year's Bud Shootout at Daytona. Because this race takes place in February, and is the first race of each new NASCAR season, drivers compete to win poles for the honor of being able to compete in this prestigious - and lucrative - event.

Provisional Starts

Being fan-friendly and commercial, NASCAR doesn't want the fans or the sponsors to be let down, and everyone is entitled to a bad day every so often. So, the powers that be instituted what's called a provisional start for drivers who did not qualify in either qualifying session. Each race allots only seven provisional starting spots. Provisional starts are designed to allow a top driver who fared poorly in qualifying to still compete in the race. Provisional starts are based on team owner points from the year before, or the current year if it's after the fourth race of the season.

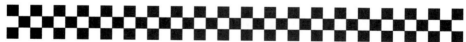

HELPFUL HINT

Because of the provisional rule, it is highly unlikely you will go to a race and not see a top star like Jeff Gordon or Dale Earnhardt. So, if your favorite racer is a top performer, avoid saying something like,
"I hope Jeff qualifies for the race on Sunday".

Happy Hour

No, this is not when team members stand in line for nachos and margaritas. It's the last practice session Saturday night for teams to make any modifications to their cars for the big race on Sunday. After happy hour, the garage is locked up until the next morning.

Sunday - Race Day

Again, the garage opens early. Some team members (called weekend warriors) arrive the morning of the race via chartered planes. The garage area is a center of activity on race morning. You'll see the teams tuning, checking and inspecting every aspect of the car.

In addition to final work on the cars, all of the drivers and crew chiefs from each team must attend a pre-race meeting. Every driver - no excuses - is required to attend this meeting, or he will have to start the race at the back of the field. If the crew chief fails to attend this meeting, he can be fined as well. NASCAR officials go through rules and track conditions. Drivers even have an opportunity to air any concerns they might have.

Driver Introductions

One hour before the race, the track announcers introduce the drivers. Again, NASCAR has the fans in mind. Drivers must also be present at this ceremony, or be sent to the back of the field for the start of the race.

HELPFUL HINT

As a fan, you want to pay attention not only to what's happening on the track but also to what's going on in the pits.

Green Flag

The car that won the qualifying round (the pole winner) starts the race on the inside of the front row in the starting lineup. This is generally considered the best place to start a race.

Once the race begins, there's no relaxing until the finish line. Unlike other sports where athletes have a break in the action, NASCAR drivers and pit crews remain focused and committed for the entire race. If you think about it, any lapse in concentration from anyone on the team could cause serious injuries to the drivers and crews involved. The exception to this continuity is a red flag which, under unsafe conditions like rain, causes all racers to pull over to the side of the track and wait.

Checkered Flag

A race is finished when all the laps scheduled for that particular event have been completed. If there's a yellow flag on the field just before the last lap, the drivers will continue running under caution until the end of the race, therefore completing all (200 for instance) laps advertised for that event.

> **FUN FACT**
>
> Bill Brodrick used to be known as "The Hat Man." He worked in public relations for Unocal 76, and during races would make sure that the winning driver and team would rotate wearing a succession of hats from their sponsors for photo opportunities.

After the race and before the winner and the top five finishers have to take their cars through another inspection (big surprise), the television crews and pit crews will swarm onto the track to congratulate the winning driver. The first thing out of the winning driver's mouth is usually a big "thank you" to his crew chief and team.

There's no questioning motorsports "fan" appeal.

Drivers aren't the only ones who need to concentrate on the race.

Then, he will thank all of his sponsors (and rotate wearing different sponsor hats).

After the race, the team will go back to the shop and prepare for the following weekend's event. The truck driver is the last to leave and has to drive home (with cars on board) for next-day car evaluations. With a season that lasts from February through November, NASCAR crews have very little free time.

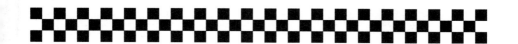

LAP 10
Open Wheel Racing
The History of CART

While NASCAR's official beginnings date back 50 years or so, Championship Auto Racing Teams (CART) can trace its roots back considerably longer to the early 1900s when the first Indy car race was held.

Today, Indy Car and CART (or Champ) cars are considered different forms of racing, but it didn't used to be that way. But before we get into the split between Indy and Champ cars, we need to discuss the history of these open-wheel cars.

Long before Big Bill France brought his own brand of stock car racing to the speed-hungry American public, Carl Fisher was responsible for bringing auto racing to the United States. In the late 1800s and early 1900s, car racing had become very popular in Europe. Fisher, along with four other businessmen from Indianapolis, believed that racing could be just as popular in the U.S., and set

Fun Fact

Although CART is considered an American series, in 1999 CART ran its 20 races on four different continents. CART races were broadcast in 19 languages to over 190 countries with an estimated 1 billion viewers.

FUN FACT

The first race at the Indianapolis Motor Speedway in 1909 was not even a car race, but rather a hot air balloon competition.

out to build a race track on a tract of farmland in Indianapolis. You guessed it. From these obscure beginnings came the Indianapolis Motor Speedway, now one of the most recognized and celebrated racing facilities in the world. However, when the speedway first opened for racing in 1909, its future didn't appear so bright. The original track surface consisted of crushed stone and tar, a slippery surface which caused many accidents to the drivers as well as to several unfortunate fans. Obviously, this did not bode well for racing, and the Speedway was forced to cancel many events.

Fisher realized he had a major problem on his hands and figured out that by laying several million bricks on the track, he could provide better traction for the cars. This strategy worked, and a new era in racing began - not to mention bringing about one of the most recognized nicknames for a track. The Indianapolis Motor Speedway became affectionately known as "The Brickyard."

HELPFUL HINT

When referring to Indianapolis Motor Speedway, you'll look like a true racing insider if you refer to it as The Brickyard.

On May 30, 1911, the famous Indianapolis 500 (Indy 500) race came to life. Until the mid twenties, however, the race featured only foreign made autos. By the end of the Depression, the American-built cars became leaders in innovation and design. During World War II, racing essentially came to a standstill with the Indy 500 shutting down for three seasons. The major transformation in Indy Car races came in the 1960s when manufacturers began adopting rear-engine designs rather than having the engine placed in the front of the car. Rear-engine cars are standard in open-wheel racing today.

Fun Fact

The rear-engine car came into its own (a significant development for Indy cars) when Jimmy Clark won the Indy 500 in 1965 in a rear-engine car.

The American Automobile Association (AAA) sanctioned all Indy Car races. (Just to be clear, Indy Car races were not only run at Indianapolis Motor Speedway. Many other tracks also featured Indy Car racing.) The racing circuit included oval tracks and road courses. In 1995, AAA conceded control over the circuit to the United States Auto Club (USAC).

By the late 1960's technology changed open-wheel racing in the United States. You could hear the buzzword "aerodynamics" everywhere you turned. The designs of the cars inevitably changed to take advantage of this aerodynamic phenomenon by becoming smaller and lighter - and much more streamlined.

> **Fun Fact**
>
> Open-wheel Indy Car racing had a major impact on NASCAR founder Bill France Sr. Apparently, France was enthralled with the Indianapolis 500.

From Indy to CART...

In 1979, a couple of team owners, including Roger Penske and Pat Patrick, decided to form a new racing series called Championship Auto Racing Teams (CART). For the next sixteen years, CART races featured Indy cars and relied on the prestigious Indy 500 to gain further recognition and credibility, officially changing the name of the series to "IndyCar" in 1992.

However, in 1995, a few of the powers that be in open-wheel racing disagreed over the technology of the cars and the economics of the league. Tony George, owner and Chief Executive Officer of the Indianapolis Motor Speedway, decided to create a competing series under a new sanctioning body called the Indy Racing League (IRL). With the split, CART lost the use of the "Indy" brand name for its cars.

Currently, there are two competing premier open-wheel racing leagues in the U.S.—CART and the IRL. CART secured many of the best drivers, while the IRL laid claim to the prestigious Indy 500 (easily the most recognized race in motorsports).

The jury is still out on whether these two leagues will bury the hatchet and again form one league. But for now, there are two leagues. One is the IRL, which races Indy Cars, and the other is CART, which races Champ cars. Champ cars currently do not meet the required specifications to race in the Indy 500. (See the Pit Stop on CART vs. the IRL.)

In 1998, a new era began for CART when the Federal Express Corporation (FedEx) became the official corporate sponsor of the CART-sanctioned series. The training ground (kind of like a minor league) for the CART FedEx Series is the Indy Lights Racing Series and the Toyota Atlantic Racing Series (both owned and sanctioned by CART).

> **Fun Fact**
>
> A Champ car can go from 0-60 mph in just 2.2 seconds (that's about how long it just took you to read this fun fact).

Open wheel racing offers excitement all its own.

HELPFUL HINT

Not all drivers start their open wheel racing careers in Indy Lights or Toyota Atlantic. Many of them get recruited to come to the U.S. after successful international driving forays in Formula One.

Fun Fact

In 1997, Janet Guthrie became the first woman to compete in the Indianapolis 500.

CART vs. IRL

Many people confuse CART and IRL (understandably), particularly when so many people call all open-wheel racing Indy Car racing. A hard core motorsports fan, however, will know most of the "current" differences between the two series. CART and IRL could merge one of these days, and some or all of these differences could be obsolete. But for now, the following are a few reasons why the two leagues don't get along.

Engines/Car:

CART teams lease their engines while IRL teams buy their engines. While this may seem like a minor difference, CART manufacturers are very proprietary about the technologies used in building their hi-tech engines and refuse to share the technology with outsiders. In fact, the engine manufacturers are the only ones allowed to work on the engines. So, if your team uses a Ford engine, as part of your lease program you'll have an engine specialist from Ford on call to work on the car's engines.

The technical specifications for Champ and Indy Cars differ. The IRL's Indy Cars are designed to be less expensive for the teams to build and maintain. Indy cars

FUN FACT

Race car driving is physically demanding. With temperatures in a car sometimes as high as 130 degrees, drivers have been known to lose 10 pounds.

only race on ovals so the construction specific to turning is not as complex as Champ cars.

CART's Champ cars run on turbocharged engines, while Indy Cars use aspirated (non-turbocharged, fuel-injected) engines. The two series also use different chassis.

FUN FACT

On a road course, a driver of a Champ car may shift an average of 3,200 times.

FUN FACT

CART racing has its own roster of racing legends who have become ingrained in the memories of American racing fans. Such names include Emerson Fittipaldi, Mario Andretti, Al Unser Sr. and Jr., and Bobby Rahal.

Location:

Indy Cars only race on oval tracks in the U.S., while Champ cars run on both ovals and road courses. Champ cars can also race outside the U.S., (although only on ovals).

The IRL believes that spectators would prefer to see racing on oval tracks, and that street and road courses are only of interest to overseas fans. CART believes that fans want to see a wide variety of racing.

Since 1995, Champ cars are not allowed to run in the Indianapolis 500, one of the most prestigious events in all of motorsports, as they do not meet IRL specifications.

In general:

Speculation continually re-emerges that the two leagues will merge. A small positive step towards reconciliation occurred in February 2000 when Chip Ganassi Racing, winners of the CART Championship series the prior four years, announced it would race at the Indianapolis 500 for the first time in five years.

LAP 11
A Week in the Life
of CART Driver
CHRISTIAN
FITTIPALDI

Christian Fittipaldi

I f you've ever thought a race car driver's life was glamorous, think again. Race drivers work hard. The racing season is one of the longest in professional sports, running from January through December, and drivers live on the road, as there are no home games. Okay, they're not required to bench press 250 pounds or run the 40 in 4.4 seconds, but make no mistake, these guys and gals are in great physical and mental shape. And, you've never seen a more dedicated and committed group of athletes in the world.

Whether you're talking CART, NASCAR, IRL or Formula One, you'll find many similarities in the personalities of the drivers

Christian with team co-owner Paul Newman

(men or women). Once you've made it to the highest levels of the sport, competition is so tough and tight, there's no room for slacking off or doubting oneself, or even having what we might consider a "normal" personal life (or any personal life for that matter).

In case you're considering going into this line of work, talk to some of the drivers and see what lies in store. Christian Fittipaldi is the driver of the Big Kmart race car prepared by Newman Haas Racing. Here he gives us a day-to-day look at what a typical week is like for him during the season. Don't let the movie-star good looks and casual, easygoing demeanor put you at ease…he's intense, competitive and passionate about racing. He also happens to be the nephew of racing legend Emerson Fittipaldi.

BB: You seem so comfortable with competitions, how long have you been racing?

CF: I've been racing since the age of 10, when I drove in my first Go-Kart race. Over the next six years, I competed in 51 races, winning 29 of them. When I was 17, I entered the auto racing circuit and shortly after, became the youngest driver to receive FIA's Formula One Super License. I entered Formula One racing in 1992 and competed there until I moved to Indy Car racing in 1995.

BB: It seems that race car drivers have very little free time during the season. Describe a typical race week.

CF: We'll start with Wednesday, because Monday and Tuesday are always a little different depending on whether a race was in town or out of town.

Wednesday:

If a race is out of town, we'll usually have to travel so we can get to the track by the evening.

Thursday:

We have our sponsor commitments, and that is all dependent on what the sponsor needs us to do and who we have to meet with. At lunchtime, we usually attend a press conference and talk about the last two weeks - how we raced, what went wrong, what went right, what adjustments were made, etc. Thursday afternoon, we'll go to the pits with the rest of the team. We'll study the car with the mechanic and go over the details of how the car is set up for the week. Everything is always a little different depending on what type of track we'll be racing at over the weekend.

FUN FACT

Christian Fittipaldi was chosen as "Single Guy of the Month" in May 1998 by *Cosmopolitan* magazine.

Thursday evening, we just try to relax and go to dinner with whoever is traveling with us. Usually, it's just me and a couple of friends. Sometimes, if a reporter needs to spend time with us for a story, he or she will join us for a casual dinner. After dinner, I just go to sleep to prepare for the long weekend ahead.

FUN FACT

Michael Andretti has appeared in three episodes of the TV comedy "Home Improvement."

Friday:

We usually get to the track no later than 9:00 a.m. and have some light breakfast at the motorhome. Breakfast is usually just cereal, fruit and some toast. I'm not really nervous at this point, there's just so much to focus on.

After breakfast, we'll go back to the transporter, and I'll usually have a couple of interviews. Then I'll go meet the engineer of the car and go over last minute things. Then it's off to the track for practice. After practice, we'll go over the car again and make some changes for qualifying.

Right before qualifying, I'll eat a little something. Then we have to qualify, which takes a few hours. After that, we'll go back to the motorhome and discuss changes for the next day. There's always something we want to change or modify, even if we had a great qualifying run.

The rest of Friday afternoon is usually reserved for sponsor commitments.

Dinner on Friday is similar to Thursday night (not very exciting). We'll go somewhere close and I'll try to have some good pasta. Even bedtime is pretty standard. I'll be in bed by 10:30 or so. If I watch TV at all, it's only for about five minutes. Usually, I'll listen to some music, then fall right to sleep. It's very easy for me to get relaxed.

Saturday:

We get to the track around 7:30 or so, and have pretty much the same breakfast of cereal, fruit and toast. Again, I'll meet with the mechanic and rest of the team. The rest of the team usually refers to Michael Andretti and his crew, as well. We need to learn as much about the cars as possible, which means that Michael and I will pay attention to not only our cars, but to each other's cars and each other's problems.

Saturday looks and feels very much like Friday. We have our sponsor commitments, then practice, then review, then more sponsor commitments. It's very routine.

Saturday afternoon after the second qualifying session, we have an all-driver briefing. Every driver has to show up for this or they fine you.

Saturday evening, we'll often go to dinner with Carl Haas and Paul Newman (owners of the team). We don't necessarily just talk racing, we'll talk about anything. And, you guessed it, I'll try to eat some good pasta and maybe a chicken breast. And definitely no alcohol. Again, I'm asleep by 10:00 or 10:30. I'm not nervous before races anymore. I've been racing for so long that, if anything, I just get anxious to get out there.

Sunday:

We're all out to the track early. Most of us stay in hotels, but some drivers (like Michael Andretti) stay in motorhomes at the track. Again, I'll have the same type of breakfast as before. I don't eat or do things for superstitious reasons, that's just what we keep stocked in the motorhomes at the track.

After breakfast, we have warm-ups, which is our last opportunity to run the car before the race. We'll go to the trailers and do some final checkups of the car. Sometimes we'll also have some quick sponsor commitments. We'll say hello to some of the people in the suites and explain our feelings about the race.

Before the race, I'll have some pasta and bread, and drink lots of water.

I'll definitely have a few jitters before the race. It wouldn't be normal if I weren't jittery.

After the race, we don't have any more sponsor commitments. We try to fly right out of the city by that night. If we win, we'll celebrate a little and have something to eat and drink. But we don't do that much celebrating because there's another race to prepare for.

Monday:

Monday is my day off. I really don't do much. And when I say I don't do much, I mean it. I go to the beach, or maybe to the movies. Most of the time, I just stare at the ceiling. Yes, stare at the ceiling.

Tuesday:

I'll work out on Tuesday. I ride the bike for about 45 minutes, and then sometimes swim and run at the end of the day. But that changes if we have overseas races to go to.

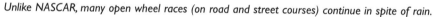

Unlike NASCAR, many open wheel races (on road and street courses) continue in spite of rain.

BB: Do you have any favorite pre-race meals when you're on the road?

CF: I don't have any "special" meals when I'm on the road, but I do like to have a good light pasta meal if I can get it, which is sometimes not all that easy depending on what city or country we're in. My favorite food in general is good, genuine Italian pasta. I eat pretty healthy, but I do have a weakness for Twix bars.

BB: What do you do to stay in shape in the off-season?

CF: There really isn't much of an off-season anymore. In 1995 and 1996, we had a little more time off, but now with 20 races a year, we have very little time at home. From May until the beginning of September, we'll sometimes be gone for three weeks in a row, and maybe have only five to ten days at home during the whole season. But, when I am at home, I like to run and swim.

It's the Pits

Among the most important factors in determining the outcome of a race is the pit strategy (determining when to take pit stops during a race and what to do in those pit stops) and physical execution of the pit stops. As pit strategy can make or break a team's prospects for victory, teams spend endless hours reviewing track scenarios that require cars to use pit stops as well as training the pit crews (see interview with pit crew coach, Andy Papa) to operate with maximum efficiency.

Why is the pit stop so important? Here's an example. Your favorite driver is in second place, neck and neck with the first place car ahead of him. He can't seem to pull ahead. He speeds up, maneuvers, tries to pass coming out of a turn but is unable to overtake his rival. His car does not have enough fuel to finish the race and he can feel from the way the car is handling (and knows based on mileage since the last tire change) that the tires are getting worn. He knows the first place car needs gas too

Life "in the pits" is tough work.

and could use a fresh set of tires. Then an opportunity arises as the first place car pulls into pit road. This is your driver's big chance. He pulls off, careening along pit road into his designated spot where he makes an abrupt stop.

The pit crew lines up on the wall ready for the driver to pull in. The driver carefully pulls in to his designated spot marked by lines on the pavement. If he misses this box, he will incur a one-lap penalty for the race. The crew leaps into action, a whir of activity. Jacking up the car, popping off the tires, putting on new tires and tightening them up in a clean, fluid motion, putting in just enough fuel to ensure a

successful finish, lowering the car, all in a matter of seconds. Hands and bodies are everywhere. As quickly as it began the pit stop ends, and the car screeches out of the pits, narrowly avoiding the pit crew members who jump out of the way. The first place opponent's pit stop has taken a couple of extra seconds, as his crew fumbles the rear tire change. Invisible to all but the expert eye, this mistake has cost the leader a few crucial seconds and allows your driver to exit the pits in first place.

Only seven team members are allowed over the wall (the wall separates the crew from pit road) during a pit stop. These team members are called "over the wall" pit crews. Each of the seven men has specialized responsibilities, as evidenced by their titles:

Jack man   **Gas-can man**

Catch-can man   **Rear-tire changer**

Rear-tire carrier   **Front-tire changer**

Front-tire carrier

The pit crew gets its direction during a pit stop from the jack man. The jack man monitors the tire changers and signals that the car is ready to leave the pit when he drops the jack. Everyone is moving at such fast speed during a pit stop it might look a little chaotic, but in a well executed pit stop, every move is timed to perfection. The jack man jacks the car up, the tire changers change tires, the gas man fills the car with gas, the catch can man catches overflow of gas and assists the gas man. If all works in harmony, a successful pit stop should take less than 20 seconds and can influence the outcome of the race.

LAP 12
The Point System
THE ROAD TO THE FEDEX CHAMPIONSHIP

CART Scoring System

Championship Auto Racing has a similar point system to NASCAR. If you ask anyone at the tracks, however, they'll say the point system is confusing and if you actually understand it, you've been at too many races and need to retire. But hey, it is one of the steps on your quest to become the Ultimate Fan.

Champ car drivers compete in the Cup Championship. The winner of the Championship not only receives the Cup, but also a $1-million dollar cash bonus.

The point system is as follows:

The top 12 positions earn points, with one additional point awarded to the pole winner. As in NASCAR, there's also a point awarded to the driver leading the most laps during the race.

FUN FACT

In 1998, Alex Zanardi (Target/Chip Ganassi Racing) became only the third driver to win the PPG Cup Championship two years in a row. The only other drivers to do so were Bobby Rahal and Rick Mears. And, to add to the success of Target/Chip Ganassi Racing, Zanardi's teammate, Jimmy Vasser, won the Championship in 1996, giving the team the Cup three years in a row.

First place	=	20 points
Second place	=	16 points
Third place	=	14 points
Fourth place	=	12 points
Fifth place	=	10 points
Sixth place	=	8 points
Seventh place	=	6 points
Eighth place	=	5 points
Ninth place	=	4 points
Tenth place	=	3 points
Eleventh place	=	2 points
Twelfth place	=	1 points

HELPFUL HINT

Remember that a driver can earn one extra point if he qualifies on the pole and another extra point if he leads the most laps. Therefore, if a driver won the race, qualified on the pole and led the most laps, he could earn a total of 20+1+1=22 points.

THE PACE CARS

Looking for a way to disprove the stereotypical image of the female driver? You know the image - the picture of uncertainty stopping in the merge lane ahead or fumbling with her makeup or adjusting the baby seat. Well, after watching, talking to, and if you're lucky enough, riding in a car with the CART Pace Car crew, you're sure to have a new image of the female driver - a steady hand hugging steep-banked curves at 140 miles per hour with a calm disposition that suggests she's sitting on her living room sofa watching television.

If you are able to see it for yourself, go to the next CART race in your area and check out the PPG Industries Pace Car team. The first thing you'll notice is all the drivers are women. The second thing you'll notice is that they're some of the most skilled and professional drivers (male or female) around.

As any race fan knows, pace cars have been around for awhile. In fact, in 1911, at the first Indianapolis 500, a pace car led the field to start the race. From then on, pace cars not only start races, but also keep the race cars in check when there are unsafe conditions on the track.

In 1979, the technicians at PPG Industries decided to combine forces with engineers and designers from a range of car manufacturers to develop superior interiors and exteriors for their pace cars. PPG could then use these pace cars to exhibit the latest innovations from all of the manufacturers involved, as well as show the quality of their high performance products. Hardcore race fans eagerly await each year's new fleet of pace cars to check out the latest innovations in technology and automotive design.

According to Jennifer Tumminelli, a Pace Car alumnus who left the program so she would have time to dedicate to her professional racing career (in American LeMans Series, the Star Formula Mazda Pro Series and the Women's Global GT Series), driving in the pace car program is a huge honor. The team consists of twelve top women drivers in the sport. The team hand-picks these women based on their performance and credentials at the tracks. These professional drivers come from all sorts of racing backgrounds including open-wheel, GT Sedan and Rally circuits. Once chosen, these women sign a contract for one year with a commitment to appear at a minimum of eight races, as well as make appearances at trade shows, auto shows and other goodwill exhibitions.

During the entire race weekend, the Pace Car crew will provide rides for a limited number of lucky individuals. Each ride is a very fast two laps around the track, sometimes at speeds as high as 150 mph. True race fans, even if they aren't lucky enough to get a ride, love to come out and see the parade of sometimes exotic and always fascinating and fast cars.

If you are one of the lucky ones to actually get a ride (the author did this at the Miller Lite 225 in Milwaukee, WI), it's worth it and will change forever your view of action on the tracks. Want to know what you're in for? Read on...

The pace car drivers tear out onto the track in their sparkling clean cars. Traffic cones are neatly placed on the side of the track and, in a very quick and systematic fashion, the assistants will lead fans to the waiting area designated by each cone and explain the process of how they will be strapped into the car. The pace car drivers don't take any warm-up laps, so as soon as they pull out onto the track, a passenger hops in and the car takes off. Immediately after the car heads down the track, the next passenger runs out to the designated spot on the side of the track to keep the line of fans moving and eliminate any downtime between rides.

Most of the fans in line will seem relatively calm about their impending ride. Some, however, (women, and yes, men) will look a little terrified when they see how fast the cars actually go, particularly through the turns. And then, of course, there will be the one wise cracker who can't help but make jokes about the women drivers and how "brave" he is to be putting his life in her hands. (Note: These guys will usually scamper off after their ride, trying to hide their white knuckles and flushed faces.)

When your car pulls up, you are strapped in (like in a roller coaster at an amusement park). Your driver will try to make you feel at ease and ask you basic questions like, "Do you like speed?" Whatever your reply, she's off, and within a few seconds you're cruising at a leisurely 140 mph. For the first three seconds you may think, "Hey, this isn't bad ... I could drive this fast," until ... your driver hits the first turn. You may look to see if she's using the brake only to observe her casually chatting with you, obviously not concerned about slowing down for the impending turn.

Remember, the pros drive differently than the rest of us. She doesn't use the brake until the end of the two laps, and that's only so she can deposit you back at the side of the track with the rest of the mortals.

According to Jennifer Tumminelli, Pace Car drivers are instructed to talk to the passengers the whole ride to make them feel comfortable. So, don't worry about them concentrating on the track... these women could cruise around at 140 mph with their eyes closed. Tumminelli also suggests not getting sick, as the pace car will not stop during your ride. A few unlucky Pace Car drivers (and the fans that had to ride in the car the rest of the day) experienced episodes such as this, but had to keep the cars moving regardless of the smell and mess!

The only disappointing part of the ride is that it's over in two laps. By the second lap, you start to feel more comfortable and even daring, and then it's over. Even so, you feel an incredible rush during those two laps. In a really small way, you get a feel for why professional drivers love to race. It's an exhilarating feeling to see the grandstands and the track rush by at blinding speeds, smell the racing fumes, feel the roar of the engine, as you climb a bank curve, and think of the unique racing history that each track holds as its special legacy.

Whether you're a hard core fan or a casual observer, have fun watching the races and enjoying the drama and excitement of motorsports' storied history.

Glossary

Aerodynamics - Referring to the effects of airflow over, under and around a moving race car, in terms of how the airflow enhances or degrades the cars' speed and/or handling characteristics.

Air Dam - A piece of the car's body that extends below the front bumper. The air dam is an essential part of car's handling package, particularly in terms of affecting downforce.

Apron - The pavement below (to the inside) of the racing surface, usually marked by a white line.

Banking - The degree of slope of the racing surface. All tracks have some degree of banking in the turns - in NASCAR, corner banking ranges from as little as six degrees (New Hampshire) to as much as 36 degrees (Bristol). Banking on straightaways ranges from perfectly flat (zero degrees) to as much as 16 degrees (again, at Bristol).

Binders - same as brakes.

Bite - The amount of tire adhesion to the track surface. (A tire that has lots of adhesion is said to have good "bite.") Adding or taking away bite is a function of the car's handling package, and is usually adjusted by using "wedge" or by changing the air pressure in the tires.

Blend Line - A line painted between the apron and the racing surface that extends from the end of pit road, giving cars an area to come up to racing speeds before re-entering traffic. The blend line often extends around the first, and sometimes, the second turn, and drivers are required to stay below the line until they attain race speed or reach a designated point on the track. Crossing the blend line prematurely may result in a penalty.

Blown Motor - A general reference to any engine failure that results in the car being unable to continue in the race. Teams are not allowed to change engines during a race, so unless the engine can be repaired, a blown engine terminates that car's participation in the event.

Carburetor - An engine component responsible for mixing fuel with air - the mixture that is burned by the engine to create power. (See also, Restrictor Plate.)

Chassis - The frame of a race car, including roll cages, engine mounts, and all hardware necessary to install the wheels and body on the car. (See also, Clip.)

Chute - Refers to a straightaway on the race track - usually one that is shorter than the frontstretch or backstretch.

Clip - Either the section of the chassis in front of the driver's compartment (front clip) or rear chassis section behind the back window (rear clip). Clips are useful in that, if damaged, they can be cut off of the chassis and replaced, thus saving the team from constructing an entirely new chassis.

Cowl - The section of the body directly in front of the front windshield that directs air to the carburetor.

Crew Chief - The chief mechanic and team leader on a race team.

Cubic Inches - A measure of volume that, in racing, refers to the "size" of the motor. In NASCAR, engines may be no larger than 358 cubic inches.

Cylinder Heads - An engine component bolted to both sides of the engine block that contains the valves, spark plugs, and ports that direct the flow of fuel to the combustion chamber. "Heads" as they are commonly called, are extremely important in making

horsepower, and are highly regulated by sanctioning bodies.

Deck Lid - The body panel that makes the top of the trunk.

Dirty Air - Air turbulence caused by other cars. Dirty air can disrupt a car's handling capability due to disruption of aerodynamic forces.

Downforce - The aerodynamic force that pushes down on a car as it moves through the air. Downforce is essential because it helps the car gain traction on the race track.

Drafting - When two or more cars race closely, one behind the other. The front car displaces the air for the group, which creates a vacuum between the cars and allows the entire group to go faster than any one car could go on his own.

Engine Block - The main part of the engine, made of cast iron (in NASCAR) or aluminum that houses the crankshaft, pistons and connecting rods.

Esses - On a road course, a series of left and right turns in succession.

Factory - Referring to direct support of a race team from an auto manufacturer. Forms of support include financial backing, supplying parts and materials, and rendering technological assistance.

Five-Point Harness - The collection of belts used to hold the driver securely in place in the race car - two belts over the shoulders, two around the upper thighs and one between the driver's legs, all coming together at one point in front of the driver's hips.

Fuel Cell - A specialized "gas tank" used in race cars consisting of a flexible bladder with foam baffling, surrounded by a metal box. The fuel cell nearly eliminates the chance of fuel spillage in the event of an accident, greatly reducing the chance of fire.

Gas Man - A crew member whose sole responsibility during pit stops is to place fuel in the car.

Groove - The best and fastest way around a race track. On ovals, the groove is established when cars leave rubber on the track, thereby creating an area that provides better tire adhesion. Many tracks have several - or multiple - grooves, while others tend to have a single groove, making passing more difficult. On a road course, the groove is generally referred to as the "line"- the quickest way around the race track.

Handling Package - The combination of factors that affect the way the car handles around the track. Components of a handling package include, but are not limited to, tire pressures, "wedge," frame geometry, panhard bar settings, sway bars, gearing, shocks, springs and aerodynamics. In addition to pure horsepower, the handling package is key in determining the speed of a car around the race track.

Ignition - The electrical system used to ignite the fuel-air mixture in the engine. Most race cars employ two ignition systems - a primary and a backup - with a switch available to the driver to change systems should one fail during the race.

"Independent" - Refers to a car owner - who often serves as the driver - without strong financial backing from a factory or major sponsor. Independents are generally single-car operations that lack many of the resources available to well-funded, multi-car teams.

Intermediate Track - An oval track that is from one mile to two miles in length. Intermediate tracks are also referred to as "speedways," and are a subgroup of Superspeedways.

Jackman - In NASCAR (where jacks are still used), the crew member responsible for jacking up the car during a pit stop.

Loose - A common term referring to a condition whereby the rear tires tend to lose traction (spin) in the corners. When a car is loose, the back end wants to slide to the outside, causing the car to spin. This condition is often called oversteer.

Lug Nuts - Large nuts required to hold the wheel in place.

Marbles - Chunks of loose rubber worn off the tires, that builds up along the outside groove near the wall. These pieces of rubber greatly reduce traction and become very slippery —— like driving on marbles.

Neutral - A handling condition that is neither loose nor tight.

Panhard Bar - A chassis component at the rear of the car that keeps the rear suspension centered with the frame. Also called a track bar, it is a key part of the handling package.

Push - A handling condition commonly referred to as tight, whereby the car resists turning in the corners, thereby causing the front tires to lose traction, "pushing" the car up the race track rather than around the corner. This condition is often called understeer.

Quarter Panel - The body panel over the rear wheels, extending from behind the driver to the rear of the car. This space is usually reserved to display the primary sponsor's logo.

Relief Driver - Any qualified driver who takes over for another after the start of the race. In NASCAR, all points are awarded to the driver who began the race, regardless of the number of laps that driver completed.

Restrictor Plate - A square metal plate placed under the carburetor that restricts the flow of fuel to the engine, thus reducing horsepower. Restrictor plates are a simple and easily-regulated means of controlling speeds at the largest superspeedways.

RPM - Acronym for Revolutions Per Minute - a measure of how fast the engine's crankshaft is turning.

Roof Flaps - A safety device incorporated in the roof of a stock car that, when deployed, disrupts airflow over a spinning car, thereby decreasing the aerodynamic force of lift, which can cause a car to become airborne.

Rubber Compound - The chemical makeup of tires, which affects how hard or soft the tire is. Generally, tire compounds are different for each track, and are also different for right-side tires and left-side tires.

Scuffs - Tires that have been run on the track for a few laps to "scuff" the tire surface, then saved for use in qualifying or during a race. Scuffing a tire allows it to heat up, which slightly changes its size and handling characteristics. When used again, it will return to the same size it was when it was scuffed.

Short Track - An oval track that is less than one mile in length.

Slick - A track condition causing tires to have poor adhesion to the racing surface. A slick track can be caused by a number of factors including the makeup of the surface itself, a sealer applied to the surface, or moisture left on the track in the form of oil, fuel, grease or water.

Spoiler - A piece of metal across the back of the car that disrupts airflow over the rear end, adding downforce and increasing drag.

Spotter - A team member strategically placed in a position to see the entire track, who communicates with the driver via radio regarding traffic and track conditions.

Stickers - Tires that have never been used. The term refers to the manufacturer's sticker found on every new tire.

Superspeedway - Any oval track one mile or greater in length. This category includes Intermediate Tracks, sometimes referred to as simply "speedways," as well as the largest tracks found at Daytona and Talladega.

Sway Bar - A chassis component that controls the amount of roll a car body has through a corner, caused by centrifugal force created in the turns. Sway bars are also referred to as anti-roll bars.

Tight - A handling condition also called a "push," when the car resists turning through a corner.

Tire Carrier - A crew member responsible for carrying new tires from the pit to the proper position on the car during a pit stop. Tire carriers work together with tire changers, and may have additional responsibilities during pit stops such as cleaning the grille or adjusting wedge.

Tire Changer - A crew member responsible for changing tires during pit stops. Most teams have a front-tire changer and a rear-tire changer employed during each stop.

Track Bar - Another term for panhard bar.

Tri-oval - A track configuration within the oval family, where a straightaway (usually the front) has a slight turn or bend. Tri-ovals are extremely popular in that they allow for better lines of sight and increased seating capacity for the fans.

Wedge - An adjustment at each of the car's four wheels that raises or lowers the car's body over that particular wheel. Adjusting wedge shifts the car's weight over each wheel, having a distinct effect on the car's handling characteristics.

Wind Tunnel - A device that simulates racing conditions by blowing air over, under and around a race car, allowing technicians to study various aerodynamic forces.

Order Form

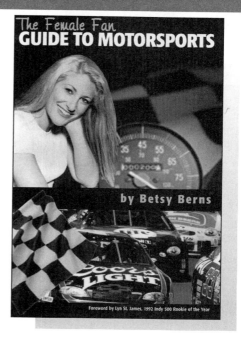

The Female Fan
GUIDE TO MOTORSPORTS

by Betsy Berns

Foreword by Lyn St. James, 1992 Indy 500 Rookie of the Year

"Betsy Berns has scored another touchdown with her latest book. Anyone interested in one of the hottest sports in the country should shift gears and grab a copy!"

Lesley Visser
ABC/ESPN

To order send this form to:
Female Fan Guides
303 East 57th Street
New York, NY 10022

Name: ....

Street Address: ....

City:...State: .... Zip: ....

Telephone:..

Sales Tax: Add $1.00 for books shipped to New York addresses.
Shipping: $3.50 per order.

Payment: ❏**Check**

Order Form

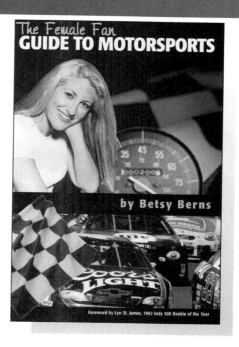

The Female Fan
GUIDE TO MOTORSPORTS
by Betsy Berns

Foreword by Lyn St. James, 1992 Indy 500 Rookie of the Year

"Betsy Berns has scored another touchdown with her latest book. Anyone interested in one of the hottest sports in the country should shift gears and grab a copy!"

Lesley Visser
ABC/ESPN

To order send this form to:
Female Fan Guides
303 East 57th Street
New York, NY 10022

Name: ....

Street Address: ....

City:...State: .... Zip: ....

Telephone:..

Sales Tax: Add $1.00 for books shipped to New York addresses.
Shipping: $3.50 per order.

Payment: ❑ **Check**

Order Form

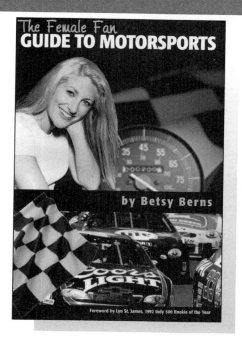

"Betsy Berns has scored another touchdown with her latest book. Anyone interested in one of the hottest sports in the country should shift gears and grab a copy!"

Lesley Visser
ABC/ESPN

To order send this form to:
**Female Fan Guides
303 East 57th Street
New York, NY 10022**

Name: ....

Street Address: ....

City:...State: .... Zip: ....

Telephone: ....

Sales Tax: Add $1.00 for books shipped to New York addresses.
Shipping: $3.50 per order.

Payment: ❏**Check**

"Auto"graphs

"Auto"graphs

"Auto"graphs

"Auto"graphs

"Auto"graphs

"Auto"graphs

"Auto"graphs

"Auto"graphs